SERVING THE STATE

Serving the State

Global Public Administration Education and Training

Volume II: Diversity and Change

Edited by

MORTON R. DAVIES
University of Liverpool

JOHN GREENWOOD
De Montfort University, Leicester

LYNTON ROBINS
De Montfort University, Leicester

NICK WALKLEY
John Moores University, Liverpool

Ashgate

Aldershot • Burlington USA • Singapore • Sycney

Published by
Ashgate Publishing Ltd
Gower House
Croft Road
Aldershot
Hants GU11 3HR
England

Ashgate Publishing Company
131 Main Street
Burlington
Vermont 05401
USA

Ashgate website: http://www.ashgate.com

British Library Cataloguing in Publication Data
Serving the state : global public administration education
    and training
    Vol. 2: Diversity and change. - (Policy Studies
    Organization series)
    1. Public administration - Study and teaching 2. Public
    administration - Study and teaching - Cross-cultural
    studies
    I. Davies, Morton R.
    351'.071

Library of Congress Catalog Card Number: 00-130117

ISBN 1 84014 075 5

Printed in Great Britain by
Antony Rowe Ltd, Chippenham, Wiltshire

Contents

List of Contributors

Pertti Ahonen
Professor of Public Administration at the University of Tampere, Finland.

Ahmed H. Al-Hamoud
Assistant Professor of Public Administration, Assistant Director of Private Sector Programmes at the Institute of Public Administration in Saudi Arabia.

Marco Cupolo
Professor of Public Administration at the Simón Bolívar University, Caracas, Venezuela.

Morton R. Davies
Professor of Public Administration and Head of Department at Liverpool Institute of Public Administration and Management, University of Liverpool, United Kingdom.

Hélène Gadriot-Renard
Directeur, Formation et Programmes at the Institute International d'Administration Publique (IIAP), Paris, France.

John Greenwood
Professor of Public Administration and Programme Director of the International Public Administration and Management Unit at De Montfort University, Leicester, United Kingdom.

Kerstin Kolam
Director of Studies, Department of Political Science, Umeå University, Sweden.

Barbara Kudrycka
Professor of Administrative Law and Public Administration at the University of Bialystok, and Rector of the School of Public Administration, Bialystok, Poland.

Tao-Chiu Lam
Assistant Professor of Public Administration at the Hong Kong Polytechnic University

Anatolii Oleksienko
Dean of Public Administration at the Institute of Public Administration, Ukraine.

Godfrey Pirotta
Senior Lecturer in Public Policy at the Department of Public Policy, University of Malta.

Charles Polidano
Staff Development Director, Government of Malta.

Lynton Robins
Co-ordinator for Public Administration at De Montfort University Leicester, United Kingdom.

Ari Salminen
Professor of Public Administration, University of Vaasa, Finland.

Frits M. van der Meer
Associate Professor of Public Administration, School of Social Sciences at the University of Leiden, The Netherlands.

Frans K.M. van Nispen
Associate Professor of Public Administration and Director of International Programmes at the School of Social Sciences, Erasmus University of Rotterdam, The Netherlands.

Nick Walkley
Lecturer in Public Management at the John Moores University, Liverpool.

Edward Warrington
Lecturer in Public Policy at the Department of Public Policy, University of Malta.

Hoi-Kwok Wong
Principal of the College of Higher Vocational Studies at the City University of Hong Kong.

Foreword
Volume II: Diversity and Change

The first volume of Serving the State focused upon the Anglo-American tradition of Public Administration Education and Training. It revealed a training capability attempting to respond to world-wide changes in the practice of public administration, to the increasing complexity of public problems, the fragmentation of public service providers, the growing complexity of public policy and rapid changes and technology. At the same time the academic discipline, faced with the public sector managerial revolution, and new global concerns and movements, has faced doubt about its disciplinary relationships with business and management and about its essential core. In many parts of the world there has been a retreat from the social sciences, and a fracturing of the discipline into functional disciplines which at crucial points may not interconnect. Consequently, the discipline in many parts of the world may become incoherent and blurred in focus. Its relevance to public sector recruitment and employment patterns depends crucially on the extent to which programmes remain professionally relevant, and - even then - to the extent to which employers attach preference to relevance. Where it fails to achieve this, an even greater responsibility falls to those providing in-service training for public sector employees.

A recurrent of the chapters in these two volumes is that Public Administration education and training cannot be divorced from changes occurring within public administration itself. In this context one factor that is often overlooked is that Public Administration educators and trainers are often themselves public sector employees, former employees, or consultants, and to this extent are not simply an observer of changing processes but a participant within it.

As a result practice in the classroom reflects much of the experience gained on the job as well as theory, and the Public Administration pedagogy is thus a part of as well as a reflection of the challenges that confront the public sector.

At the same time the nature of a country's education system also has an impact. For example, in a developing country where educational opportunities are few, or where rapid transition can render existing skills and knowledge obsolete, there may be insufficient qualified and experienced trainers and educators available to support changes in public administration. Another crucial factor is the value placed by society and governments on public administration itself. In a job market offering relatively few opportunities for public sector employment, or significantly lower salaries than available in the private sector, the raw material for training and education in the classroom may not be come available.

This second volume explores how far these experiences and challenges relate to other traditions and contexts including: the French and Islamic traditions, the Netherlands and Scandinavia, Latin America, small island states, former Communist countries such as Poland and the Ukraine, and others -notably China - undergoing rapid economic change. The studies have been chosen to include not only contexts and traditions not covered in the previous volume, but also to reflect geographical diversity. Thus while the first volume drew extensively on experience in Britain, North America, Africa, and Australia, this second volume contains contributions from Asia, France, Latin America, Scandinavia, the Middle East, and eastern Europe. It does not claim to provide a comprehensive picture of global Public Administration education and training, but does present a picture which covers salient experiences and traditions and allows wider conclusions to be drawn. The volume ends with a concluding chapter which attempts to draw together some of themes and conclusions supported by the individual studies in the two volumes as a whole.

Morton R. Davies (University of Liverpool)
John Greenwood and *Lynton Robins* (De Montfort University, Leicester)
Nick Walkley (Liverpool John Moores University)

January 2000

1 Development, Issues and Challenges: Public Administration Education and Training in China

TAO-CHIU LAM AND HOI-KWOK WONG

Introduction

Xu and Xu (1996) suggest that 'every civil servant should study Public Administration'. In the new civil service code promulgated in 1993, training has been made a regular feature. Under the new system, not only are newly recruited civil servants required to attend training courses offered by administrative colleges and the like but serving civil servants are also required periodically to receive training. Public Administration, moreover, has become a core ingredient of training programmes. The National School of Administration (NSA), a training institution that rivals the privileged position of the well-established Central Party School, has been established, although, as we argue below, it is still grappling for a role and struggling to gain some influence in the making of China's bureaucratic elite.

The introduction of a new civil service system in 1993 has been the impetus to civil service training in China, but the rising importance of educating and training public officials preceded this. The backbone of all leadership within communist China is the cadre; 'individuals who may or may not be party members who hold positions of leadership within the party, state, army, communes or any other organization' (Walker, 1981). No sooner had reform begun than the Chinese government recognised that the cadre force, which under Chairman Mao did not have adequate education and professional skills, needed to be re-educated and re-trained. As a result, cadre training and Public Administration education had grown rapidly. One of the first texts on Public Administration, published in 1985, sold more than one hundred thousand copies (Liu, Xu and Xu, 1996). In about a decade, more than one hundred texts on Public Administration were published, many of which have sold quite well. It is said that at any one time, several million people are studying Public Administration in many different institutions in the country (Liu, Xu and Xu, 1996).

The extraordinary growth of Public Administration education in China calls for an explanation. One and a half decades ago Public Administration as an academic discipline simply did not exist in China. Together with other social sciences, Public Administration as a discipline disappeared from universities from the early 1950s. The discipline was only rehabilitated in the 1980s. What accounted for its rapid expansion since the 1980s? What are the main features of Public Administration education in China? How far is China's Public Administration education different from Public Administration in Western countries? What are its main problems and challenges?

This chapter addresses these questions. Our main argument is that while the Public Administration discipline has re-emerged to meet the challenges presented by China's reform and awesome administrative problems, its responses have been generally disappointing, and it now risks being pushed aside as irrelevant. Every civil servant is required to study Public Administration, but scholars in China remain puzzled about what Public Administration really is. To a certain extent, this is the same problem plaguing Public Administration scholars across the world, but in China, the identity problem is further compounded by two other factors. First, as a result of the discipline's disappearance for three decades and its short history, China is still awaiting its Woodrow Wilson and Dwight Waldo. Public Administration is not just a discipline in search of an identity, it is also a discipline in search of properly trained scholars. Second, and more importantly, China's Public Administration scholars are not free to study whatever they find interesting and worth studying: Public Administration is too political and too intertwined with the fate of the polity to be a matter of academic inquiry. Public Administration education, while carried out on an immense scale, now risks becoming a ritualistic and formalistic process that lacks substance. These characteristics not only help define the unique character of Public Administration education in China, they are also the root causes of its problems and challenges.

This chapter analyses the above issues through a detailed examination of the key training institutions, Public Administration scholars, trainers and trainees, training programmes and methods, and finally, the outcomes from training and Public Administration study. Towards the end of the chapter, we discuss the limited role of training in the making and selection of the bureaucratic elite in China. Although a high-level National School of

Administration has been established, and many people have chosen to compare it with the ENA in France, in fact it has far less influence. Before proceeding to these issues, however, we will briefly discuss the development of Public Administration as an academic discipline in China.

Developing a Public Administration Discipline to Serve the State

To scholars such as France Schurmann and Harry Harding (Schurmann, 1968; Harding, 1981), organisational issues and the bureaucracy were at the centre of political struggle and ideological disputes during the Maoist era. China under Mao was also a typical case of an administered society as defined by Kassof (1964). However, the importance of administration and the centrality of bureaucratic issues in political struggle and ideological disputes did not encourage the development of a discipline focused on such matters. Chairman Mao did not see much value in social sciences so, in the early 1950s, he abolished all social sciences, with the partial exception of anthropology, from universities. On the eve of reform, all former social scientists had either left scholarship altogether, or moved to natural science, or refocused their academic pursuit to Marxist-Leninism or what was broadly called scientific socialism.

Suddenly, with the death of Chairman Mao and the arrest of his most radical followers, the Gang of Four, the nation refocused its development strategy and begun to relax the emphasis on ideological purity and political correctness. After more than a decade of Cultural Revolution, the country's administrative system was in a dismal state. The bureaucracy had been altered so frequently and in such an irrational way that it barely functioned, if at all. The bureaucracy was filled with many unqualified cadres as a result of the practice of giving priority to 'red' (political loyalty) over technical expertise and competence. During the early years of the reform moreover, the situation deteriorated, because the regime needed to rehabilitate hundreds of thousand of cadres purged during the Cultural Revolution. Most of the rehabilitated cadres were not up to the demands of economic reform and modernisation. The accommodation of the rehabilitated cadres not only bloated bureaucracy further, it also created an administrative system that bordered on paralysis. In one central ministry, for example, there were as many as 28 deputy ministers, making decision-making extremely slow and difficult if not impossible. Many cadres were too old and weak to walk, but they continued to hold on to power. China needed a retirement system, but was yet to develop one because of bureaucratic opposition (Manion, 1992).

As the political leaders started to grapple with these administrative problems, they came to the view that a discipline of Public Administration would help. In the early 1980s, several social science disciplines including political science had been created, and as an institutional expression of this development, the Chinese Academy of Social Sciences (CASS) was established (Halpern, 1988). Seminars and lectures on Public Administration had been organised by the newly found Institute of Political Studies under CASS. But the milestone was 1984 when state agencies and key political leaders directly took the initiative by calling for the development of a discipline of Public Administration. With strong support from the state, suddenly China had a Public Administration discipline. Some scholars were instructed to move from other areas to the new discipline, while others, perceiving good prospects for the new discipline, joined voluntarily.

It is often said that in China social science scholarship has always been required to serve the state. The Chinese state rehabilitated such disciplines as economics, sociology and political science in the late 1970s because it thought that these discipline would help the country's modernisation (Halpern, 1988). The same consideration, of course, is true for Public Administration, but its association with the state is closer than with other academic disciplines. Firstly, two state agencies, namely the Secretariat of the State Council and the Ministry of Labour and Personnel, were directly involved in the establishment of the discipline. Second, following the call for the establishment of a Public Administration discipline in 1984, a national Public Administration Association was established under the Secretariat of the State Council, with the Secretary-General of the State Council as its first president. Across the country, sub-national public administration associations were established under local government bodies. By the early 1990s, a network of public administration associations was already in place, serving as an important organisational instrument for Public Administration study and research.

Public Administration study, therefore, has developed more as a state activity than as an area of academic inquiry in China. This feature was also evident in the nation-wide effort to establish cadre training colleges and administrative colleges to train state cadres and civil servants, and to re-orient the focus of the party schools. As early as the 1980s, there was a call for establishing an ENA-type national school of administration. Yuan Baohua, then Deputy Director of the State Economic Commission and concurrently President of the People's University of China (now renamed the Renmin University of China) in Beijing, lent strong support to the idea and formed a preparatory group at the university. However, this idea did not make much progress until 1988, when it was decided that China should establish a national network of administrative colleges. In 1993, when the civil service code was promulgated, it was also decided to establish a National School of Administration. Now the school is headed by a State Councillor and placed directly under the State Council having the same administrative rank as a ministry. Bureaucrats and ex-bureaucrats filled the leadership of the NSA, with academics playing only a subordinate role. Administrative colleges have also been established at the provincial level and below across the country.

An Instrumental Discipline

Public Administration, many people in the discipline argue, is different from other social sciences in that it is more relevant to real problems to which it is able to provide solutions. It is different from political studies in that it does not touch so directly on sensitive political issues. These perceptions explain why initially key political figures and state agencies took a keen interest in the discipline's development. The Secretariat of the State Council, responsible for the functioning of the administrative system, and the Ministry of Labour and Personnel, charged with personnel system management and reform, have been directly involved in defining the foci of Public Administrative study and research in China. The national Public Administration Association is established under the Secretariat of the State Council, with its presidency held by the Secretary-General of the State Council. In the 1980s, there were substantial interests in improving administrative efficiency and administrative re-organisations. Many people in the field thought that Public Administration study would make great contributions to these enterprises. For example, the theme for the first conference organised by the National Public Administration Association was China's administrative system reform. More than two-thirds of the members of public administration associations are practitioners.

Public Administration as an academic discipline in China has been closely associated with the growing emphasis on training cadres and civil servants in recent years. The newly established colleges across China have become the main institutional bases for the study of Public Administration. An interesting result is that many people who do not study or research in the field have identified themselves with the discipline of Public Administration. Many leading cadres of administrative colleges (e.g. party secretaries and presidents) hold leading positions in public administration associations and even author texts on the subject. This reflects the tendency for the study of Public Administration to be identified with training cadres and civil servants. Many people change their research fields because they have taken up leadership positions in administrative colleges. A leading official of a major administrative college in China is an example of this. Before taking up the position in the administrative college, he was head of the Communist Youth League in a university and had no connection with the study of Public Administration at all. Upon becoming the vice-president of the administrative college, he claimed to be an expert on the subject.

Another interesting phenomenon is that many officials in state agencies also identify themselves with the discipline. While it is perhaps natural that officials from state personnel agencies are closely associated with the study of Public Administration, it is odd that officials who are responsible for secretarial services, logistics and other supporting services are also strongly identified with the discipline. Under the auspices of the National Public Administration Association, for example, there is a research association for the administration of logistic services. As another example, a Deputy Secretary-General of the State Council took up the presidency of the National Public Administration Association after retiring from the state bureaucracy. In 1998, the National Public Administration Association had a new president. Like his predecessor, the new president is also a retired cadre from the State Council. Perhaps more tellingly, before retirement he was head of the State Council's Estate Bureau.

Scholars in China always point to the frequent flow between officialdom, universities and research organisations as a source of the discipline's strength, arguing that practitioners and scholars have something to teach each other (Xu and Xu, 1996). However, there are far fewer flowing from campus to officialdom than the other way round. Our impression is that officials do not have much respect for scholars and what they have offered or can offer. On the other hand, because there is a dearth of Public Administration scholars, and also because scholars court close association with leading officials, the flow from officialdom to campus has been common. The Remin University's Public Administration department, for example, has appointed several high-ranking officials as their adjunct professors. The NSA not only has a State Councillor as its president but all of its deputy presidents are either incumbent or retired bureaucrats. Senior officials are often invited to give lectures in administrative colleges. Because Public Administration scholars have not developed much expertise this is not surprising. It is often said that these officials bring with them valuable and contribute to the healthy growth of the discipline (Xu and Xu, 1996), but exactly how far these officials are able to contribute to the study of Public Administration is far from self-evident.

The discipline of Public Administration aroused a lot of enthusiasm and hope when it re-emerged in the 1980s. In more recent years, enthusiasm has declined considerably and there is a widespread feeling that the discipline has failed to make much impact on China's administrative reforms and policy making, dealing a heavy blow to the claim for relevance. Furthermore, in comparison with other social sciences, the discipline's scholarship is also disappointing. Many books and articles that have received national awards contain little more than abstract principles (Guo and Yu, 1992). Given the discipline's short history and the many constraints it is facing in China, this is not surprising. The recent decline of enthusiasm and the emergence of disillusionment may be good for the discipline: when it is not expected to be immediately relevant to government, and treated as an area of academic discipline in its own right, the discipline can perhaps grow more healthily, and without too much political intervention.

Problems and Challenges

It is far from certain how, and whether, the discipline will develop in China. There are still many worrying signs. Public Administration scholars have generally not acquired the necessary expertise and autonomy: they continue to depend on association with officials and on official recognition for their status and identity. Another worrying sign is that, institutionally speaking, Public Administration is represented more in the administrative colleges and cadre training colleges than in universities. Since the crackdown which followed the pro-democracy movement in 1989, universities in China have given a greater emphasis to developing Public Administration programmes, but, as we will discuss below, study of the discipline has still been predominantly associated with training and educating public officials. Lastly, and most importantly, Public Administration scholars have failed to identify an area or a set of questions in which they can claim expertise.

As Greenwood, Robins and Walkley point out in the first volume, Public Administration is such an all-embracing area that even in western countries, 'the subject field of Public Administration has long been recognised as presenting enormous problems of focus and definition' (Greenwood, Robins and Walkley, 1998). In China, Public Administration scholars have identified as their main focus such issues as the proper roles of the state, the state structure for a socialist market economy, and how the state can strengthen macro-management (Liu, Xu and Xu, 1996). As these issues have also been of fundamental concern to economics and other disciplines, there is naturally a question about what distinctive light Public Administration can shed upon these issues. Although the same question has never ceased to plague the discipline in the West, in China this problem is more acute in the sense that Public Administration scholars, generally having done little empirical research and studied few real administrative problems, often only echo the policies and rhetoric of policy makers.

Bo (1998), a professor of the NSA identifies the following areas as the weaknesses of the study of Public Administration in China:

- it is still bound by the framework developed for studying Public Administration in Western countries;
- many publication and texts plagiarise one another, indicating the lack of rigour of many scholars in this field;
- there are very few comparative studies;
- it has not adequately absorbed the findings and knowledge of other disciplines;
- it has exclusively emphasised efficiency and neglected other values important in public administration;
- the study of the philosophical foundations of administrative behaviour and phenomena is weak;
- scholars are excessively concerned with abstract theories and principles, and pay scarce attention to real administrative problems;
- some important areas, e.g. public finance and economic management, have been neglected;
- the larger society with which public officials and their policies interact has also been neglected;
- research methodology is simplistic and backward.

Bo's article marks a general dissatisfaction with the status of the study of Public Administration in China. On the other hand, it is instructive to learn that, like many of his colleagues, the author has also listed a large set of agenda issues for the discipline to pursue. These include, for example, administrative philosophy, the proper functions of government, controls over government power, the rule of law and the scope of the public domain. Two particular challenges flow from this conception. First, as already mentioned, if Public Administration is viewed as such an all-embracing discipline, what is the unique contribution of Public Administration scholars and research? Second, China's political reality still presents considerable barriers to some of the remedies proposed. For example, there is insufficient empirical research, not only because scholars in China have not seen its value and are often not trained in research methods, but also because research may have far-reaching political implications for individual officials and organisations.

In one respect, however, direct state patronage has been a blessing. The leadership virtually re-established the entire academic discipline overnight, and in the last decade the study of Public Administration has grown rapidly. It comprises a national network of public administration associations, cadre training and administrative colleges, a modest establishment in universities, and a large body of Public Administration scholars and teachers. However, state patronage has also prevented the discipline from enjoying any real independence. It has inhibited the development of its intellectual maturity and - by inculcating an overriding concern with 'hot topics' determined by state leaders (Cheng, 1995) - has defeated the aspiration to offer well-informed policy advice to policy makers.

Institutional Framework for Public Administration Education and Training

The key institutions responsible for studying Public Administration, and educating and training public officials in China, are respectively Public Administration and politics departments in universities, and administrative colleges, cadre training college and party schools. Some of China's most prestigious universities, like Peking University, Remin University of China, Fudan University, Nanjing University and Zhongshan University, among others, have set up Public Administration programmes. These programmes are either offered in a department of Politics and Public Administration, or in an International Politics department, or in a separate Public Administration department. As of the end of 1998, there were more than twenty Public

Administration programmes in universities (Bo, 1998). Qinghua University, China's premier science and engineering university, drawing on its strength in training senior civil servants from the Hong Kong government for many years, is also in the process of establishing an administrative school to tap the growing and lucrative business of cadre training

China has a formal and hierarchical degree system, which governs the issuing of formal academic qualifications. Due to historical reasons, Public Administration, even after its development gained official support in the reform era, has not received formal recognition in the institutionalised degree system; indeed, most social sciences have also not been formally recognised. Thus, for example, a political science major is formally called a degree in law, while Public Administration is only one of several fields under the political science major. One can only claim a specialisation in Public Administration with a major in political science while receiving a degree in law. One consequence is that Public Administration has been hosted mainly in political science departments in those universities that were known to be relatively strong in political science, for example, Peking University, Fudan University, Zhongshan University and Wuhan University. In recent years, a separate public administration department or school has been established in Remin University, Jilin University and Shenzhen University.

A Lucrative Source of Income

Apart from undergraduate degrees, some universities also have postgraduate programmes in Public Administration. The longest running of these is the programme at the Remin University, which has been offered since 1986. Initially Remin University offered the programme with assistance from Canada's McGill University, but after a few years this assistance ended and since then, the university has offered the programme with little outside assistance. In 1995 a number of other universities (Peking, Fudan, Jilin and Wuhan) were granted approval to offer MPA degrees.

Just as China's economic growth during the reform era has occurred mainly in the non-state sector, in Public Administration in universities the greatest growth has been in what in the West is called the self-financed programmes. In China, all universities are owned and funded by government. Each year the state controls the number of students which each university and programme can admit. However, universities and departments are allowed to take in additional above-quota students. These students do not take the competitive nation-wide entrance examination and pay higher tuition fees. Normally these students are serving cadres who are seeking academic credentials. The higher tuition fees are not a problem for such students as they are paid by the organisations for which they are working. As funding for universities has declined and become somewhat erratic universities and departments have found these self-financing programmes an important source of revenue. Very often the staff's salary, bonus and other welfare depends greatly on income from such programmes.

Public Administration has recently become popular as a programme for study. Many serving cadres seeking to improve their academic credentials believe that a Public Administration programme is closely related to their experience and work. The potential market is huge, as the public bureaucracy has a strong emphasis on higher academic qualifications (Li and Bachman, 1989; Li and White, 1990). Some universities have become very entrepreneurial in tapping this market. Peking University and Remin University, for example, offer Masters-level Public Administration programmes not only in Beijing (where they are located), but also in various provincial capitals. They send staff members to these outposts during weekends and vacations to teach courses and supervise students.

Apart from programmes leading to degrees, other universities also offer Public Administration as a subject. According to one estimate, in the early 1990s more than 500 departments and colleges provided Public Administration teaching in China (Guo and Yu, 1992), although a large proportion of these were in the cadre training and administrative colleges which are discussed below.

Party Schools, Administrative and Cadre Colleges

The most noticeable institutional development during the past two decades in China is the rapid expansion of administrative colleges and cadre training colleges, and the re-orientation of the party schools. Although precise figures are lacking, the number of administrative colleges, party schools and cadre colleges broadly identified with Public Administration education and training in China exceeds by a large margin the formal universities that provide programmes in this field. Of these three types of institutions, the party schools and cadre training colleges have a longer history, and each have an integrated network across the country.

Party schools are established from the centre to the county level in three ways: at each level of administration, some functional ministries and some large state enterprises (DZRG, 1995). At the end of 1989, there were about 2,700 party schools with 38,000 full-time teaching staff at and above the county level. Before the reform era, the party schools mainly focused on political and ideological indoctrination and education, and this emphasis has not disappeared entirely during the reform era. However, several factors have worked to move the party schools closer to the teaching of Public Administration, not the least of which has been the decline in the importance of politics and ideology as fields of study in China during the reform era. A section on Public Administration teaching and research was established in the Central Party School in Beijing, for example. The party schools system has also made contributions to specific fields in Public Administration, one of which is leadership science. However, the importance of the party school system lies in its role in cadre training. In 1993 a new civil service code was promulgated which led to the establishment of administrative colleges in a number of provinces. Some party schools found it necessary to offer courses in Public Administration as a strategy to cope with the possible competition from the new administrative colleges. Indeed in some localities party schools actually amalgamated with the new administrative colleges. As a result, Public Administration now is a core area in many party schools.

For much the same reasons, Public Administration has also been of increasing importance in cadre colleges, of which there are two main types: administrative cadre colleges and technical cadre colleges. These two types of cadre colleges, numbered at 250 and 2,800 at the end of 1989, had a teaching staff of 18,000 and 48,000, respectively. The party schools and cadre colleges together had the capacity to admit 1.4 million trainees at any one time (DZRG, 1995).

Compared with the party schools, the administrative colleges established by the new civil service code have had far less of an ideological and historical burden to carry, and have thus been able to focus more strongly on Public Administration. The civil service code requires that state civil servants should receive training both when first entering the civil service and periodically thereafter. At the peak of the administrative college network is the NSA, which has an establishment of 400 and has the capacity to train 1,000 civil servants. By 1998 most provincial units in China had also established administrative colleges. Some administrative colleges have also been established below the provincial level. For example, Guangdong Administrative College has set up ten 'campuses' in cities across the province.

Institutionally speaking, Public Administration education and training in China exhibits some distinctive features. The close link between political science and Public Administration is still found in universities, but outside the universities, Public Administration has flourished as an independent entity. Separate Public Administration departments have been established in most administrative colleges and party schools. Of course, this separation by no means suggests that the discipline of Public Administration has become an independent area of intellectual inquiry. It serves instead as an indicator of the immense and continuing domination of the party-state on Public Administration education and training.

China's Public Administration Scholars and Trainers

The above section suggests that China has already created a comprehensive institutional framework for educating and training public officials. As a result of the extraordinary institutional growth, there has been a huge demand for Public Administration scholars and, more generally, trainers. We have shown earlier that most of China's Public Administration scholars did not have formal training in the field; nor have they done much research in Public Administration. In some cases, many people claim Public Administration as their specialty because they were institutionally associated with administrative colleges and training organisations, or because their former experiences in the state bureaucracy (such as supporting services) were seen, often erroneously, to be related to study of the discipline. In this section, we examine the background of both the trainers and trainees more closely.

With the rehabilitation of the discipline in the early 1980s, after previously being banned for three decades, China found itself having only a few senior scholars with formal training or research experience in Public Administration or related disciplines. To fill the demand for teachers, a large-scale reassignment of teachers was undertaken from dwindling fields to this newly-expanding discipline. Crash courses to introduce the fundamentals of Public Administration to prospective teachers were organised in the 1980s by a few surviving veterans. As a response to what is still a dearth of qualified teachers, many universities and teaching institutes have drawn on experienced practitioners as adjunct professors, particularly to lecture to in-service participants on short-courses related to their portfolios.

The career of Huang Daqiang, who had made great contributions to the development of Public Administration as a discipline in China, is a telling one.

Before his death, he was Director of the Research Institute of Public Administration at Remin University. His academic background was in scientific socialism and he was originally with the university's Department of International Politics. Before that, he was an editor with *Red Flag*, official magazine of the Central Committee of the Communist Party of China. Due to his enthusiasm and good connections, he was able to secure strong support for the new institute, including overseas help in teaching and research.

Since its foundation in 1986, Huang's institute has graduated a number of Masters students, some of whom now teach Public Administration in universities, party schools and administrative colleges across the country. Other universities such as Peking, Fudan and Jilin, which are relatively strong in political science and Public Administration, have also sent graduates to teach Public Administration elsewhere.

The number of students studying Public Administration in China varies greatly, depending on how Public Administration education and training is defined: for example, whether we count all cadres attending short training courses or only full-time students enrolled on courses approved by the educational authorities. As noted above, the number of full-time students is small compared to those on self-financed programmes targeted at serving cadres, who have grown further in numbers in the last two years as a result of the streamlining of the central government bureaucracy. To reduce the social and political impact of cutting back on a large number of serving civil servants, the central government has arranged with universities to admit a large number of the surplus staff to study for degrees and Public Administration has been a very popular subject. Self-financed programmes have grown rapidly also because, in keeping with centuries-long Chinese tradition, higher academic qualifications have almost become a necessary condition for advancement in the bureaucracy. On the supply side, as we have seen, universities and training institutions in China are more than eager to provide these self-financed programmes.

The growth of self-financed programmes also reflects the relaxation of education control in China. While the government still exercises tight control over regular courses, the total number of students, and the level of tuition for these courses, has given greater freedom to universities to engage in self-financed programmes. Over the years, these and more generally other commercial undertakings, have become not just a matter of demand but a matter of necessity. Without them, China's universities could hardly survive.

Even before the passing of the civil service code in 1993, a series of major decisions had been made to strengthen cadre training. The objective was to train every single cadre at least once and, thereafter, to train them periodically. Various types of short-term training courses were developed and by the end of the 1980s about 97 per cent of cadres at and above the county level had received some kind of training. For the most part, of course, such trainees do not specialise, nor seek a degree in, Public Administration. Public Administration is usually only one of the subjects in the training curriculum, although it is increasingly seen as one of the major courses to be offered in training programmes.

The regime under the leadership of Deng Xiaoping also aimed at raising the academic qualifications of the entire cadre force. Again, the scale of developments was quite colossal and improvements were, in fact, quite impressive. In 1978, cadres having college, senior high school, and junior school or lower education were 18.2 per cent, 32.3 per cent and 49.5 per cent, respectively. By 1987, the percentage having attained college education had risen to 32 per cent, and senior high school or equivalent to 47.5 per cent, with a corresponding significant drop in the percentage of cadres having only junior high school education or lower (DZRG, 1995, 348-9).

What is Being Taught?

This short account of the study of Public Administration in China, coupled with the extraordinary institutional growth of the past one and a half decades naturally leads one to ask: is there much substance to this huge demand and supply of Public Administration and training? What is being taught in Public Administration programmes? What do the trainees study? Given the huge resources committed to Public Administration education and, particularly, training in China, it is also important to know what this leads to in career terms. This last question will be examined in a later section. The present section deals with what is being taught and how.

It should be clear from the discussion above that party schools and administrative colleges have dominated Public Administration education and training. Training, in particular, entails a very broad scope, encompassing ideological, theoretical and political indoctrination, programmes studying the party line and new policies, job-related and technically-oriented courses, and the study of Public Administration itself. Added to this complexity is the fact that cadre training has also often been confused with cadre education, the meaning of which is even broader because it includes also the improvement of the academic qualifications of the cadres (DZRG, 1995, 327-61). As such, it would be a mistake to equate the importance of education and training of public administrators with the growth in importance of the study of Public Administration.

As in many Western countries (Greenwood, Robins and Walkley, 1998), Public Administration is only one of the many subjects offered in the party schools, cadre colleges and administrative colleges. The typical training programme in party schools includes such conventional courses as Marxist theory and philosophy, socialist economics, and theory of party building. In recent years, there has been a greater emphasis on courses such as leadership science and policy-making studies. Also many party schools have also initiated programmes to keep leading party-state officials informed of the latest technological developments and the operation of the world economy.

While it is often suggested that the training programmes should take many forms - which should emphasise creative participation and involvement by the trainees, discussion between trainers and trainees, and among the trainees themselves - in practice most training programmes are in old-fashioned lecture form. Field visits, simulations, seminars, case discussions and direct observation seem to be encouraged, but with the exception of field visits, other forms of training activities are few and far between. Field visits are welcomed by trainers, but they often fade into sightseeing. In 1994, a State Council document called for a halt to many such activities because they are not much more than sightseeing and represent an improper use of public revenues.

In the universities the curriculum of Public Administration education reflects the short history and under-development of the academic discipline. A recent study (Wang, Guo and Ma, 1998) suggests that Public Administration programmes in different universities in China have much in common. The courses offered fall into the following six categories: political science, management, Public Administration, public policy analysis, law, and basic skills. The study also finds out that these programmes have a large proportion of courses in political science and management, with few courses on Public Administration and economics. It also revealed that there is an almost complete absence of public finance courses on Public Administration programmes. This study compared Public Administration programmes in Chinese universities with those of North American universities, and suggested that China's Public Administration scholars should also develop more courses on skills and empirical analysis and integrate more with other disciplines. The study also identified key defects of Public Administration programmes in China's universities and pointed out some desirable changes which, it was believed, were necessary.

In an earlier article (Lam and Wong, 1996), we have noted that four main features are evident in the discipline of Public Administration in China:

- a pragmatic orientation which stresses that Public Administration scholars should study practical problems and should be able to provide practical advice to practitioners to improve policy efficiency and effectiveness;
- a dearth of empirical study on administrative phenomena and problems (which, when placed alongside the strong demand for relevance and pragmatism, is puzzling);
- a managerial approach to Public Administration (with a peculiarly Chinese policy- administration dichotomous view);
- a tendency to focus overmuch upon questions of political economy.

All these features are interrelated. The managerial approach obviously reflects the bent on pragmatism and earlier unrealistic expectations of the potential contribution of the study of Public Administration. Managerialism is also a strategy by which scholars in China could stay away from sensitive political issues. We have argued that, with regard to the relationship between politics and administration, Chinese scholars seem to hold two contradictory views. On the one hand, they argue that politics and administration are inseparable (which is in line with the party's view), but on the other they take the Wilsonian stand that Public Administration basically is a field that is or should be free from politics.

This latter view has prevented Public Administration scholars in China from addressing how state administration has been linked to politics and the political system, and has therefore hampered the growth of empirical and rigorous study of administrative problems. Another closely related problem is the failure to establish a domain for the discipline of Public Administration. As pointed out above, in China Public Administration is often viewed as a grand discipline encompassing all other disciplines. Certainly, this is not a problem unique to China because in other countries Public Administration is also viewed as encompassing 'virtually the entire activity of the modern state, ... [and it] has long been recognised as presenting enormous problem of focus and definition' (Greenwood, Robins and Walkley, 1998). But in China, this view is also a reflection of the interconnectedness and holistic nature of the socio-economic and political change. Apart from establishing departments and programmes in universities, public administration associations and administrative colleges, Public Administration as a discipline in China still faces the arduous challenge of establishing its domain and identifying its unique role among competing and more established disciplines such as economics.

With regard to teaching methodology in universities this has been mainly in the form of 'chalk-and-talk' lectures. It appears that tutorial sessions and seminars have not been widely used, although there has been a strong emphasis on case studies with considerable efforts having been made to compile cases from both China and other countries (Huang and Xu, 1988). To the best of our knowledge, there have not been any internship programmes.

Bureaucratisation of Training Activities

One of the most noteworthy features of cadre training in China is the high level of bureaucratisation of training activities. The sprouting of administrative and cadre training colleges noted above is a typical example of bureaucratisation. Training activities have been organised bureaucratically, in that common programmes and curriculum have been prescribed for the whole country. Various deadlines have also been set for different types of training. But the most important evidence of the bureaucratisation of training activities is that training agencies have assigned official texts for trainers. Trainees are also required to pass examinations, which are based almost entirely on these official texts.

Initially, these initial texts were prescribed by the Ministry of Personnel. This was, however, resisted by the personnel officials at the provincial level because they also wanted a share of this huge market for texts. Many texts were written (or to be more exact, edited) by leading officials of those personnel agencies with the authority to determine the form and substance of training activities. For example, one Vice-Minister of Personnel has edited more than a dozen texts on Public Administration and China's new civil service system. At the provincial level, the names of key personnel officials often appear in texts even though they did not participate at all in the editing and writing process. Normally, officials assign their books as texts for the training classes directly under their control. Because official texts are assigned, training activities often turn into a formalistic process of memorising the official syllabus and passing written examinations. Trainees that we have interviewed typically think that training activities are too ritualistic, and that they are neither stimulating nor useful.

What do Public Administration Study and Training Lead to?

There is no direct link between university study in Public Administration and service in the government bureaucracy, as in many other countries. Considering the fact that public administration has far from attained the status of a profession, this should not be surprising. The civil service recruitment examination introduced in recent years covers a wide range of topics and there is no reason to expect Public Administration graduates possess any significant advantage. The history of Public Administration education in Chinese universities is also too short to establish any clear relationship between it and the careers of its graduates. At the same time, because many serving officials are enrolling onto Public Administration programmes on a part-time basis, there will be more and more officials possessing degrees in the subject.

There seems to be a closer link between training of serving officials and promotion, but this relationship is more complicated than at first it might appear. It is true that at present training has become quite institutionalised and regularized, but it is misleading to attach too much importance to the effect of training on bureaucratic promotion. Training in party schools and administrative colleges will be a salient factor only if enrolment in a training programme is restricted and competitive, or performance in a training programme affects the outcome of promotion exercises. Neither of these two conditions applies to China. Under the existing framework promotion decisions are made first and the selected candidates are then sent to institutes for training. Training therefore has almost no effect on personnel decisions. In China's existing cadre management system where important personnel decisions are controlled by the party, it is hard to imagine that training institutes could have great influence.

Yet there seems to be one exception to this rule. In recent decades, young cadres deemed to have potential have been carefully groomed and sent to attend training courses in party schools. It is said that such training prepares these young cadres for faster promotion and more important positions. This kind of training has been closely monitored by the party's organisation departments, and seems to have considerable impact on the trainees' career prospects. In the past, this was the preserve of the party schools. The new NSA has reportedly been struggling to gain a foothold in this kind of training, but the extent of its success is still not clear and it would be difficult to conclude that it has assumed anything like the role of ENA in France

Conclusion

The main thesis of this chapter is that the rehabilitation and development of Public Administration education and training in socialist China has occurred as a result of direct state patronage. The study of Public Administration and in particular the training of public administrators, at least in an institutional sense, has grown at a rapid pace. It is quite an achievement that now every single serving civil servant has received some training, and every one of them is required to acquire some knowledge of Public Administration. However, it is also important to note that these were results not of natural development, but of administrative fiats.

Against this background, a critical issue is what the study of Public Administration has delivered or can deliver. This question is particularly important given the pragmatic value and relevance expected of the discipline in China. The enthusiasm for the discipline quickly subsided, following the realisation among scholars and practitioners that there were no ready and scientific answers to many of China's chronic administrative pathologies. Soul-searching and a concern for identity have replaced the initial optimism. Similarly, in the training of public administrators there is much room for improvement. The establishment of administrative colleges is just the first step. There are more demanding challenges for long-term capacity building and institutional growth. As far as the role of training is concerned, China appears to come closer to the British approach than the French; the administrative colleges in China just have a role in training, not one of selecting and making an elite (Greenwood, Robins and Walkley, 1998).

References

Bo, G. (1998), 'Zhongguo Xingzhengxue: wenti, tiaozhan yu duice', (Public Administration in China: Problems, Challenges and Our Measures), *Zhongguo xingzheng guanli*, 1998, vol.12, pp.4-7.

Cheng, L. (1995), 'Senior and Middle Ranking Civil Servants Training at China's National School of Administration', paper presented at International Association of Schools and Institutes of Administration Annual Conference, Dubai.

DZRG. (1995), *Dangdai zhongguo renshi gongzuo (Personnel Work in Contemporary China)*, Dangdai zhongguo chubanshe, Beijing.

GPJZFJ (1993), *Ganbupeixunjiaoyu zhengcefaguijingxuan (A Selection of Policies and Regulations on Cadre Training and Education)*, no publisher given (in Chinese).

Greenwood, J. Robins, L. and Walkley,N. (1998), 'Global Public Administration and Training: Common Themes or National Differences?' in M.R. Davies, J. Greenwood, L. Robins and N. Walkley (eds), *Serving the State: Global and Public Administration Education and Training,* Ashgate. Aldershot, UK, and Brookfield, Vermont, USA.

Guo, B. and Yu. X.(1992), *Xingzheng guanli yanjiu gailan (An Overview of Research on Public Administration),* Sanxi chubanshe, Taiyuan.

Halpern, N. (1988), 'Social Scientists as Policy Advisers in Post-Mao China: Explaining the Pattern of Advice', *The Australian Journal of Chinese Affairs,* no. 19-20, pp.215-240.

Harding, H.(1981), *Organizing China,* Stanford University Press, Stanford.

Huang, D. and Xu, W. (eds) (1988), *Zhongwai xingzheng guanli anli xuan (A Selection of Public Administration Cases from China and Other Countries),* Zhongguo renmin daxue chubanshe, Beijing.

Kassof, A. *(1964),* 'The Administered Society: Totalitarianism Without Terror', *World Politics,* vol.16, pp. 558-75.

Lam, T. and Chan, H.S. (1995), 'The Civil Service System: Policy Formulation and Implementation', in C.K. Lo, S. Pepper, and K.Y. and Tsu (eds), *China Review 1995,* paras. 2.1-2.43.

Lam, T.C. and Wong, H.K. (1996), 'A Discipline in the Shadow of the State: Public Administration in China,' *International Journal of Public Administration,* 1996.

Li, C. (1994), 'University Networks and the Rise of Qinghua Graduates in China's Leadership', *The Australian Journal of Chinese Affairs,* no.32, pp.1-30.

Li, C. and Bachman,D. (1989), 'Localism, Elitism, and Immobilism: Elite Formation and Social Change in Post-Mao China', *World Politics,* vol. 42, pp.64-94.

Li, C. and White. L. (1990), 'Elite Transformation and Moderr Change in Mainland China and Taiwan: Empirical Data and the Theory of Technocracy', *The China Quarterly,* no.121, pp.1-35.

Liu, Y., Xu, W. and Xu, L. (eds.) (1996), *Zhongguo xingzheng kexue fazhan (The Development of Administrative Science in China),* Zhongguo renshi chubanshe, Beijing.

Manion, M. (1992), 'Politics and Policy in Post-Mao Cadre Retirement', *The China Quarterly,* no.129, pp.1-25.

Schurmann, F. (1968), *Ideology and Organisation in Communist China,* University of California Press, Berkeley and Los Angeles.

Waller, D.J., (1981), *The Government and Politics of China.* 3rd edn, Hutchinson, London.

Wang, L., Guo, X. and Ma, J. (1998), 'Zhongxifang gongong xingzhengxue zhuanye kecheng tixi bijiao', (A Comparison of Public Administration Programs in China and Western Countries), *Zhongguo xingzheng guanli,* 1998, no.7, pp.22-25.

Xu, S.and Xu, L. (eds.) (1996), *Zou xiang zhuoyue de zhongguo gongong xingzheng (Toward Excellence: China's Public Administration)*, Zhongguo renshi chubanshe Beijing.

2 The Different and the Similar: Public Administration Education and Training in Finland

PERTTI AHONEN AND ARI SALMINEN

Introduction

In many respects Finland is the odd one out among the Nordic countries. Yet she is also an inalienable member of her group of countries. Unlike the Scandinavian Nordic countries Sweden, Norway, Denmark and Iceland, whose heritage includes the glorious Viking era, Finland has been drawn into the global scene only since the 12th century as a melting pot of Orthodox and Russian influences from the East and Roman Catholic and later Lutheran Swedish influences from the West. Linguistically she remains predominantly a non-Scandinavian country. For 95 per cent of her population of 5.1 million the mother tongue is the Fenno-Ugrian Finnish, distantly related to Hungarian, and only five per cent of her citizens report the Indo-European Germanic language of Swedish as their first language. The language of Finland's second indigenous minority of about 3,000 people, Sami, is also of the Fenno-Ugrian stock.

Ninety-eight per cent of those Finns who identify themselves with a religious denomination resemble their Scandinavian neighbours in that they are Lutherans and adherents to its version of the Protestant ethic. However, unlike her neighbours Finland also has a second and a well visible albeit small indigenous Orthodox national church which is traditionally strongest in Finland's east. Since the 1920s the latter church has been a Greek Orthodox instead of Russian Orthodox. There are also other differences that prevail in the emphases of habitus and mentality between the closed, *sachlich* and serious Western Finns and the more open, sociable and easy-going Eastern Finns. This concerns, in particular, the East's Karelians.

Finland is the only EU country to share a common border with the Russian Federation, and that a long one of no less than 1,200 kilometres. Finland also trades actively with Russia after a severe economic recession in 1992-5, although the uneven transitiòn of Russia continues to cause problems. Finland is the easternmost bridgehead of the EU and a spearhead in EU cooperation with north-western Russia. The transitional country where Finland's presence is strongest is still Estonia, with which the large majority of Finns share a common Fenno-Ugrian linguistic background. It is to Estonia that the bulk of Finnish investment in transitional countries has been lately oriented.

Despite its many unique characteristics, Finland is undeniably a member of the family of the Nordic countries. This also includes the special feature that together with Sweden, Norway and Denmark she belongs to those of Europe's countries that are populationwise rather small, in the range of four to nine million. Together with Sweden and Norway Finland is a Nordic country with a large land area and sparse population and quite a harsh climate.

The economic, social and administrative systems of Finland and the other Nordic countries are nowadays more similar than dissimilar. The political systems have also lately grown increasingly alike, as Finland has been rapidly abandoning her previous constitutional tradition of a semi-presidential government. Note that although in the period 1809-1917 Finland was part of the Russian Empire, she never was subordinate to Russian legislation. Instead, she was under her own domestic legislation derived from 18th century Swedish constitutional laws that the Russian emperor in 1809 allowed her to preserve as Russia's sole efficient autonomous Grand Duchy.

All the five Nordic countries have always been countries with predominantly market economies. Yet the public sector has had an important role in supplementing the market; there have been elaborate systems of institutionalised public welfare service provision, and there has been a high concern with equal access to public services by the citizens. There are also fundamental similarities between the Nordic countries in their public sector development policies typically emphasising decentralisation, the nurturing of equality in public service provision, a considerable emphasis upon municipal self-government, and a pragmatic attitude towards the adoption of the tricks of the New Public Management

(Ahonen & Salminen, 1997). The fact that unlike her Scandinavian neighbours, there was never a social democratic predominance in Finland kept Finland's public sector the smallest in the Nordic countries. Very paradoxically, it was only the economic depression of the early 1990s which led to an evening-out of those differences but despite that Finland was the Nordic country probably pursuing the most determined neo-liberal policies by that time.

Together with the Netherlands, Belgium and Ireland, all Nordic countries have in the modern era applied fairly liberal recruitment policies to public administration jobs. Here they are in direct opposition to France, which is the stronghold of an elaborate career civil service in Europe (Temmes, 1997). Other European countries than those mentioned usually apply a mixture of liberal recruitment and strict career elements. This background is also important for analysing education and training in Public Administration. However, it remains debatable to what extent the overt Finnish and Scandinavian anti-élitism, motivated by explicit reference to democracy and equal access to civil service positions for all who hold the required level of education, has really succeeded. It is debatable, in particular, to what extent the declared anti-élitism served to fend off undesirable secrecy in recruitment, implicit as opposed to quite explicit recruitment criteria, and a frequent role of political party affiliation as a recruitment criterion (Temmes & Salminen, 1994).

During Finland's advent to its own state entity, since 1809 and including the first decades of her independence since 1917, a large part of leading civil servants were lawyers. However, already before World War Two demands arose to achieve differentiation in the expertise available in top and expert civil service positions (Ahonen, 1994)

The only true tendency that evolved towards Public Administration training in Finland before World War II was the establishment of the Social Science College in Helsinki in 1924. There, degrees comparable with the Bachelors came to be awarded in the field of Public Administration (generic, municipal and tax administration), social welfare (especially insurance and social insurance) and social studies (e.g. journalism and social work). Similar developments are known to have taken place in the same period in Sweden.

Evolution and Expansion of Finnish Education Related to Public Administration

The Establishment of Education in Public Administration in Finland

During World War II in 1944 two important developments took place related to Finland's Public Administration. First, the Finnish Ministry of Finance established an Organisation Department and the post of Commissioner in Public Administration as the leading civil servant of Public Administration development. The first Commissioner was Urho Kekkonen, later Finland's long-time president of 1956-81. Second, in 1944 the University of Helsinki established the Social Science Faculty with the explicit aim of achieving differentiation in the professional background of top and expert civil servants. The Faculty was and is *valtiotieteellinen tiedekunta, statsvetenskapliga fakulteten, Fakultät der Staatswissenschaften,* and not meant to be an ordinary social science faculty.

From the point of view of civil service education the new faculty turned out to be something of a disappointment. It generally took an orientation towards standard Western social sciences. It is true that a particular degree, a Master in Administrative Studies, was offered to provide for the expert needs of practical administration. However, the degree was not felt to come up to expectations, which is why it was discontinued at the beginning of the 1960s.

Parallel developments to those at the University of Helsinki took place in the Social Science College. There, the first full professors' positions were established as of the late 1940s, and masters and later doctoral degrees began to be awarded. The very first of the professors' chairs later to be included in administrative sciences were established in 1950 in Municipal Politics at the College.

In 1960 the College moved from Helsinki to Tampere, and in 1965 it was expanded to comprise a sufficient number of faculties to be upgraded into the University of Tampere. A small Swedish-speaking Social and Municipal College evolved in Helsinki in the 1950s, awarding bachelors degrees.

At the stage that the Master in Administrative Studies was discontinued at the University of Helsinki, as if in compensation an Associate Professor's position in Administrative Studies was established at the same university, in

1963. Soon the discipline of political science at that university differentiated into three orientations: general political science, international politics and administrative studies. All had and continue to have a common core, and the differentiation takes place after one and a half to two and a half years of studies. Partially or fully separate masters and doctoral seminars have come to be arranged for each subfield.

In 1965 the University of Tampere created a new Faculty of Economics and Administration to supplement the Faculties of Social Sciences and the Humanities. In the first faculty, three orientations towards teaching and research were defined: first, an orientation of mathematics, statistics, computer science and philosophy; second, a small business school unit and a Department of Economics; and third, four disciplines and four corresponding departments in the administrative sciences. At the same time, the Masters, the Licentiate (lower doctoral) and the Doctoral degrees in the Administrative Sciences received their first statutory definition. The tradition of the Social Science College was continued in that several Vocational Training Faculties persisted, turning out degrees most closely resembling a Bachelors in several specialisations including the traditional ones falling close to Public Administration. However, there was no direct continuation from the vocational faculties to the new academic faculty, but the students with a vocational degree had to pass the general entrance test.

The disciplines and departments defined in the administrative sciences at Tampere in 1965 were:

1. Social and Economic Ecology, later named Regional Studies
2. Public Administration, since 1994 named Administrative Science
3. Public Law, not to train lawyers but administrative specialists
4. Municipal Politics.

The two first disciplines were new creations without direct precedents in Finland. The third discipline had had its equivalents in the Social Science College in addition to the fact that public law was by that time also really well established in lawyers' training proper. The fourth discipline had been a masters, licentiate and doctoral discipline in social science (*Sozial-wissenschaft*) before its definition as one of the administrative sciences.

The four new departments soon merged, only to start splitting up again quite soon. In 1994 the teaching positions in the sole remaining Vocational

Training Faculty were merged with the academic departments. This affected the latter three of the four departments in the administrative sciences. After a transitional period the previous vocational Bachelors degrees were discontinued. The discontinuation was in part compensated by the 1994 introduction or re-introduction of Bachelors degrees in the teaching programmes offered throughout Finland in the social sciences. The main motivation for this step was to make it explicit on the European scene that the Finnish Masters degrees involves more than Bachelors degrees in the other member states.

The Rationale for Establishing Public Administration Education in Finland

University education in the field of Public Administration is particularly widespread in Finland. Up to and including doctoral degrees it is offered nowadays in no fewer than seven of Finland's ten full-scale multi-faculty universities (Appendix 1). Moreover, and quite unlike the other Nordic countries, there is no tendency in Finland to perceive that field of education as part of or subordinate to political science, *statsvetenskap* and *Staatswissenschaft*. This is the case despite the contrary indications of a national evaluation of the Finnish administrative sciences by a Finnish and a Swedish political scientist (OPM, 1994).

The overt identification of the Finnish administrative sciences with such values as equality, social welfare, democracy and the public interest is weak rather than strong, although these sciences continue to deal mostly with public sector problems. Instead of identifying themselves as political sciences, or even nurturing a strong interest in questions of public policy-making, their typical approach is managerial or otherwise technocratic. Their typical scientific profile ranges from scientism to generic organisation and management research. Signs of the times in the administrative sciences in the mid-1990s have included the change of the disciplinary name Public Administration into Administrative Sciences with the exception of one university, and the upgrading or the establishment of several new teaching disciplines as if to better meet the contemporary demand and satisfy the dominant professional interests.

There has not been any single rationale behind founding and upgrading disciplines related to public administration in Finland:

- The Bachelors education in fields related to Public Administration at the Social Science College since the 1920s had the rationale of providing public authorities with low- to medium-level civil servants. The same rationale was behind the establishment of the Swedish-speaking Social and Municipal College in the 1950s.
- The establishment of the Social Science Faculty at the University of Helsinki in 1944 had as part of its rationale the enhancement of civil service training over and above legal training.
- The establishment of the education in Tampere was spurred on by threats felt in the 1950s by the interest groups close to the Social Science College of an imminent merger with the University of Helsinki. The national policies of expansion of Finland's national network of universities and the preference at Tampere to have a local university provided the constituency with a suitable counterpart. The rationale of accomplishing civil service–oriented education outside legal education had also survived throughout the 1950s. To provide for this end, the College had the considerable record of forty years of Bachelors education in the field, and the social sciences were also strong there. Finally, there was a desire to provide education meeting the needs of both the national government, the regional administration and the local governments.
- The rationale behind the establishment of administrative sciences at Åbo Akademi was to accomplish in the Swedish-speaking community of Finland on a smaller scale what had arisen in the majority Finnish-speaking community and located at Tampere.
- As part of the national policies of higher education, the Vaasa Business School was expanding at the turn of the 1970s and the 1980s from a university college towards a full-scale multi-faculty university. An interest arose to include also the administrative sciences in the Faculty of Social Sciences that was being established. Regional interests in the Vaasa region welcomed the expansion and provided some start-up funding. This was analogous to certain developments in Tampere.
- The expansion aims of the University College at Kuopio specialising in education in medicine met professional aims to upgrade education in nursing to include academic degrees. As administrative and managerial tasks are part and parcel of the work of many

professionals with a nursing background, Health Care Administration was established as another discipline in the administrative sciences.

- Regional needs have provided an important part of the rationale for the establishment of the newest entrants in the administrative sciences at the University of Lapland and the European Union's easternmost University of Joensuu.
- The expansion of economic and business thinking in matters related to the Finnish public sector has provided the rationale for establishing several new academic disciplines in the administrative sciences or upgrading existing disciplines to include masters and doctoral degrees.
- The feeling in Finland's national government that administrative sciences were too weak in the country's capital led to a considerable strengthening of Administrative Studies at the University of Helsinki, with two new temporary but still long-time professorial positions in 1994.
- In addition to Kuopio, professional upgrading has provided a particular rationale for the establishment of the discipline of social and health care administration in Vaasa and the subdiscipline of security (police) administration in Tampere.

Institutionalisation of Finnish University Education Related to Public Administration

Annex 1 describes the way in which Finnish administrative sciences falls into teaching disciplines. The annex also lists the universities offering each discipline, the result units involved, the number of professorial faculty, and the year of establishment of the discipline at that university.

- The Tampere departments and disciplines are now once again slowly moving towards a merger. They are already included in the new statutory School of Public Management, which could become their common result unit and even a new faculty, with the concommitant abolition of the present departments.
- What in Tampere is separated into four major disciplines in the Departments of Administrative Science and Local Government

Studies outside Tampere comprise the single discipline of Administrative Science, and at Åbo Public Administration. This is no necessary weakness for the universities following the integrated model.

- At the Vaasa Faculty of Social Sciences the role of the administrative sciences has been predominant. This has first concerned, above all, the discipline of administrative science. This interestingly resembles the situation in one of the global strongholds of Public Administration, namely the Maxwell School at the University of Syracuse in the United States.

- Despite its orientation towards questions of health care in a university started as a medical university college, the actual substance of the Kuopio disciplines is not very different from what is encountered in the Finnish administrative science at the other universities.

- Despite its position within political science, Helsinki Administrative Studies shares an orientation that resembles that of the discipline of Administrative Science especially in its Tampere variant. Note that there also used to be an orientation in administrative studies in the discipline of political science at the University of Turku. However, this orientation was merged with ordinary political science at the turn of the 1980s and 1990s. Yet this has not prevented the latter department from housing scholars who study Public Administration, although neither they nor their work can be covered by this analysis.

- Note the Swedish-speaking Bachelors degrees in the field of Public Administration in the Swedish Social and Municipal College of the University of Helsinki. The College was annexed to the University at the turn of the 1980s and 1990s. Yet, unlike the Vocational Training Faculty of Tampere, it was not organically merged with the Faculty of Social Science but has maintained an autonomy. Here, the language aspect has been decisive in keeping the Swedish-speaking College autonomous from the bilingual University of Helsinki, where the Finnish language markedly predominates.

- Since 1995 the Finnish administrative sciences have shared one of Finland's 100 plus doctoral schools with special funding from the Ministry of Education and the main funding of basic research from the Academy of Finland. The formation of this doctoral school to include only the administrative sciences and only them as outlined in this study is one indication of their contemporary legitimate boundaries.

Relationships of disciplinary dominance within Finland's administrative sciences are rather vaguely articulated. Some relationships of dominance do exist, however:

- In public law, belonging to the administrative sciences, legal disciplines exert an unquestionable dominance, and an analogous situation exists in tax law.
- To the extent that regional studies is not yet completely differentiated from its origin in geography (as it in many respects is not), a relationship of dominance prevails.
- In the Helsinki unit of the Finnish administrative sciences, as well as partially in the Åbo Akademi unit, political science has a position of dominance, more or less.
- The Vaasa unit comes closest to a situation of a first predominance of administrative science as a generic discipline.
- In Tampere none of the eight full masters, licentiate and doctoral disciplines in the administrative sciences has dominance. For some of them administrative sciences is only a label with a lesser substantive import. It is also relevant that the Tampere discipline of Administrative Science has a much narrower scope than the same discipline in the other universities offering it, as at Tampere there are three other sovereign disciplines in the same domain. Tampere also has no less than six (but after Vaasa's full establishment of regional studies only five) unique disciplines in the administrative sciences which are not offered elsewhere in Finland. In some cases they exist in no other country. This creates the situation where the disciplinary basis remains narrow and thin, even if disciplinary autonomy may be made absolutely strong in the institutional sense.
- The disciplinary origin of the professors in the core governance and Public Administration part of the Finnish administrative sciences reveals some further aspects of disciplinary dominance. That field includes the disciplines of administrative science; financial management and public sector accounting; municipal politics; and

Public Administration. Among the professors of those disciplines, at the beginning of 1998, six had a doctorate in political science, four in Public Administration, three in municipal politics and three in some other discipline (economics, business accounting and regional studies, one each).

- Questions of disciplinary dominance also include the extent to which competence in one discipline suffices for competence in another discipline in competition for professorial positions. Political science continues to provide competence in administrative science, Public Administration, municipal politics and, within the limits of supplementary qualifications in economics or accounting, in financial management and public sector accounting. Administrative science and Public Administration continue to provide at least a partial competence in political science and municipal politics, but municipal politics, in particular, may not suffice for a considerable competence in political science. Competence in administrative science and municipal politics can be expected to arise from health care administration and social and health care administration and also vice versa, although less so. The two latter disciplines, on the contrary, hardly imply an acceptable scientific competence in political science. Unexpectedly, regional studies has turned out to be a source of highly valid competence in the discipline of administrative science, although the reverse is in no way true. To an extent the latter circumstance is an upshot of a very high output of doctoral degrees in regional studies and a very low corresponding output in the Tampere discipline of administrative science and its predecessor Public Administration. The situation can be mended only very slowly. The first doctor in almost fifteen years having worked at the department will received the degree in 1999. This is different from the other departments of a comparable size that have been able to show a rather solid comparable doctoral output over the years.

There is no doubt about an almost complete disciplinary sovereignty of the Finnish administrative sciences within the Finnish universities. They are not subordinate to the disciplines of business studies or law. They are not subordinate to political science at all with the exception of Helsinki.

However, there is no doubt about the heavy intellectual reliance of the Finnish administrative sciences upon numerous disciplines outside their own domain, from political science to law, the disciplines of business studies, sociology, geography and others.

In the Finnish administrative sciences a marked - and in the case of Tampere extremely marked - disciplinary differentiation combines with a lack of intellectual independence. This hints at a situation where these sciences are the beneficiaries of really novel research in that they themselves were the origin of new research results that exerted strong influence over and above the delimited empirical domain in question. This conclusion receives indirect support from any comparison of the capability of Finnish administrative scientists to attract citations as recorded in such a well-reputed database as the Social Science Citation Index. There, in comparison with their colleagues in similar fields in the other Nordic countries, the Finns are badly underrepresented. Most of them seem to be scholars who prefer to be make themselves and their work known only in the national arena. One must wonder if this feature has not also exerted an influence upon the education and training provided, including the doctoral training and results or lack of them in that training.

The Process and the Contents of Finnish University Education Related to Public Administration

The education we deal with in this study is made up only of university education aiming at Bachelors or postgraduate degrees. Our analysis is simplified by the fact that there are really no Bachelors degrees proper offered by any of Finland's new polytechnics so far. This is why we can deal solely with academic degrees proper. If in the future direct routes are opened from the polytechnics lately upgraded from vocational colleges, the situation will change radically.

Finland's university system is relatively exclusive in that the completion of a matriculation examination (an Abitur) at the end of upper secondary school is typically not a sufficient guarantee for a university place. The characteristic entrance criterion is success in a competitive entrance test. The student also receives points on the basis of good results in key disciplines of the matriculation examination. There are separate entrance requirements to all the disciplines in the administrative sciences, including the requirements that are different at different universities to gain admission to the same discipline. The typical entrance test is rather general in that it is based only upon the command of the applicant of one or two basic books in the target discipline. The typical test involves essay writing and answers to questions concerning details of the book or books prescribed for the test. Although the apparent role of chance is great the junior teachers responsible for the entry test questions and the grading of the answers solidly believe in the validity of the test.

The students are admitted to complete the Masters degree, that is, there is no separate entrance test for the Bachelors degree. The students must in any case complete all of the Bachelors requirements as part of the Masters degree studies, but they can choose whether they actually take the certificate of the interim lower degree or not. They can also choose to leave the university after they have taken their Bachelors. This has been rather rare at least in the administrative sciences, nor is it encouraged by the universities.

A limited number of students in the Finnish administrative sciences - perhaps 10-20 per cent - are admitted in ways other than through the entrance test. These are people who have already pursued considerable studies in their target discipline in open university courses or who have completed other studies making them eligible. There are also small quotas for people who wish to gain the right to pursue studies in a given discipline without taking a degree. Later on they may apply in the former category or take the general entrance test.

There is a *numerus clausus* for admittance to the doctoral studies. This rules out the students with the lowest grades in their Masters degrees. However, they can try to improve their degrees to gain admittance.

The target length to complete the Masters degree is about four and a half years full-time. There are records of average completion times of five to six years in the administrative sciences. The students should be able to complete the Bachelors degree in three to three and a half years of full-time study.

The Finnish result units in the administrative sciences – mostly departments, in some cases faculties – have nowadays a vested interest in promoting the timely completion of Masters and Doctors degrees by their students. After a transitional period lasting until 2003, the departments will receive their entire basic funding on the basis of their fulfillment of their objectives in two criteria. Two thirds of the allocation will be based upon the fulfillment of a target output of Masters degrees, and one third will be based upon the fulfillment of a doctoral degree output target. The departments will receive no benefits for exceeding their output targets. Nor do they receive anything on the basis of their output of Bachelors or Licentiate degrees nor the minor field studies offered to students from other departments. The latter three result criteria do receive some attention in the determination of the rather small part of the departments' resources which are allocated by the universities themselves at their discretion.

Annex 2 includes selected descriptions of courses of Finnish university education in the administrative sciences at the two universities where these sciences are at their strongest, namely at the University of Tampere and the University of Vaasa. It is basically the same domain which is covered at both universities, namely a core area of traditional Public Administration as it has received a contemporary interpretation in Finland. It arises only from the high differentation into various teaching disciplines at Tampere that a somewhat narrower area can be covered in the overview provided in the annex. Neither the Tampere Masters degrees in the teaching disciplines of municipal politics (local government studies) nor municipal economics (local public economics) are explained, although the respective fields are in principle also ones covered by the Vaasa discipline of administrative science.

Within limits, the characterisation of the discipline of administrative science as defined and taught at the University of Vaasa is also indicative of the same or the corresponding discipline in Åbo and Lapland. The Vaasa situation is, admittedly, less indicative of the situation at Helsinki and Kuopio.

The fundamental difference between Tampere and Vaasa is the complete separation at the former university of an administrative science discipline with an economic emphasis. This, in turn, deprives the traditional root discipline of Tampere of all contents in economics and accounting. It can also be noted that in the economically oriented Tampere discipline there are discernible signs of a European and policy orientation, whereas the other Tampere discipline is a representative of a generic organisation and management orientation. An observation that can be made of the Vaasa situation - and *mutatis mutandis* Åbo, Helsinki and Kuopio - is the fairly general orientation of the education offered and the fairly wide scope that the education wishes to cover.

Employment of Finnish Public Administration Graduates

There is something of a paradox in that the share of graduates in the Finnish administrative sciences recruited into central and local government has traditionally been lower in Finland than the comparable share in many other academic fields. For instance, graduates in education, medicine and several of the natural and humanistic sciences go almost entirely into the public sector.

Up to 90 per cent of students from the University of Tampere who graduated in the administrative sciences in 1967-1982 were in the latter year employed mostly in the public sector. One fourth worked in the national government (its central, regional or local branches), 57 per cent in the municipal sector; seven per cent at universities and research centres, one per cent in church parishes of Finland's two national churches, two per cent in various associations and seven per cent in the private sector, mostly companies. The respective alumni who had graduated in 1980-1993 worked in the year 1994 still mostly in the public sector, up to 79-83 per cent, depending on how the alumni who were employed by public enterprises are categorised. Eighteen per cent were employed by the national government, 40 per cent by the municipal sector, thirteen per cent at the universities in administration or research jobs, four per cent in public enterprises, eight per cent in a category *other public sector*, four per cent in associations, twelve in private companies, and two per cent in other jobs (Mälkiä et al., 1997). A clear change had taken place in that the share of the public sector as an employer had clearly decreased and that employment in the other sectors had considerably increased.

The latest available data on the recruitment of Finnish university graduates in the field of Public Administration and nearby fields continue to concern the University of Tampere. There, a survey was conducted of students who had graduated in the years from 1994 till 1996. The survey continues to be partially representative of Finland as a whole. In that year the Tampere output of graduates in the administrative sciences was probably one half of the national total. The graduates were asked their situation one year after completion of their degree (University of Tampere, 1998. This is the data source of all the analyses below).

Although there is the common situation of a drastic decrease in recruitment to the public sector, graduates in the administrative sciences as an aggregate have found employment relatively well (Table 1). It is possible that private business has become recruitment-averse to no lesser degree than the public sector, which would explain why the recruitment of business school graduates has not been extremely easy either. The fact that in the administrative sciences both the share of those permanently employed and the share of the non-employed is rather high hints at a polarisation between various disciplines in those sciences. This can be elaborated as follows.

Table 1   Employment of University of Tampere Graduates of 1994-6 in Certain Disciplinary Fields (one year after graduation)

Field of Degree	For comparison: Business (Accounting, Marketing, Management, Business Law)	For comparison: Social Scientists, non-Administrative Scientists	Social Scientists, Administrative Scientists
	Percentage		
Permanent employment	58	30	42
Temporary employment	33	52	35
Unemployed jobseeker	6	7	11
Not at work, other reasons	3	11	12
Total	100	100	100
N	177	420	156

Among the administrative sciences, a very mixed view of the core Public Administration disciplines is provided by the survey. The discipline of administrative science is the loss leader in that one third of the graduates of 1994-6 was not working. The share of unemployed jobseekers is close to the overall national figure, but a few times higher than the corresponding national figure for the entire population of occupationally active Finns. In the discipline of administrative science the high figure of the *other* cannot derive from massive let alone promising entry into doctoral training, as that discipline has not excelled in such activities. Hidden unemployment which has gone unreported is the likeliest reason for the latter figure. Financial administration and public sector accounting, the other direct inheritor of the venerable discipline of Public Administration, in turn, shows next to excellent results both in the share of graduates who have found permanent employment in the adverse labour markets of 1994-7 and in the absence of the *other* group. The only reservation concerns the not very low unemployment figure, which prompts the question whether the discipline should select its students in a more systematic way to ensure the full employability of the graduates. However, given that the output of the discipline was nineteen, the unemployment share of 10 per cent involves only two people and does not rule out chance producing the apparently rather high figure of the unemployed.

The discipline of Municipal science also fares rather badly in employment. In 1994-6 there was not yet any output of Masters degrees in the same department's discipline of municipal economics, which has a similar profile as financial administration and public sector accounting. In the Department of Regional Studies and Environmental Policy the latter discipline has no Masters degree output to report in the period in question. public law is something of a positive anomaly. It is evident that it meets keen competition from public law for lawyer training. Its graduates also continue to seek and find employment in the public sector. However, public law in the administrative sciences fares well, although in that discipline there is a differentiation into a high share of those permanently employed on the one hand and on the other those keeping out of working life for inexplicable other reasons. Tax law is a special case: in 1994-6 it largely turned out Masters degrees for people who had taken the prior special Bachelors in tax law and were typically already very firmly established in various jobs. The degree output is also too small to justify any bold conclusions (Table 2).

Table 2 Employment of University of Tampere Graduates of 1994-6 According to Discipline (one year after graduation)

Field of Degree	Administrative Sciences					
	Regional Studies	Administ— rative Sci- ence	Financial Managem- ent	Public Law	Tax Law	Munici- pal Politics
Employment	Per cent					
Permanent	29	37	53	61	50	36
Temporary	43	30	37	21	50	40
Unemployed	14	15	10	7	0	10
Not at work, other	14	18	0	11	0	14
N of graduates	28	33	19	28	6	42

Field of Degree	Business			
	Business Account- ing	Marketing	Management and Organisation	Business Law
Employment	Per cent			
Permanent	73	50	57	70
Temporary	25	42	30	30
Unemployed	2	5	10	0
Not at work, other	0	3	3	0
N of graduates	48	46	30	10

Field of Degree	Social Sciences, non-Administrative Sciences (selection)				
	Social Policy	Social Work	Political Science	Interna-tional Politics	Sociology
Employment	Per cent				
Permanent	36	32	23	32	25
Temporary	43	57	57	57	52
Unemployed	13	5	3	5	9
Not at work, other	8	6	17	6	14
N of graduates	39	86	35	86	44

Data on other disciplines of the University of Tampere provide background for conclusions regarding the Tampere administrative sciences (Table 2). It seems that an "accounting turn" had taken place in Finland by the period considered. Business accounting graduates were the leaders in finding employment, with a similar situation in financial administration and public sector accounting as regards the administrative sciences. The situation in the venerable discipline of social policy resembles that in the no less venerable discipline of administrative science, suggesting an overproduction of degrees in a saturated market. Social work and tax law resemble each other in turning out Masters degrees by upgrading previous Bachelors degrees in markets far from saturated. Social work is comparable with financial administration in that the former discipline is not, unlike the latter, an outgrowth of a previous master discipline, namely social policy. To a much lesser degree financial administration and public sector Accounting has also been able to upgrade previous Bachelors degrees into Masters degrees.

The dominant share, 77 per cent, of graduates in the administrative sciences had in 1994-6 continued to find their employment in the public sector (Table 3). This is a high figure, but it is considerably lower than the 90 per cent or so of a few years ago, as reported above. The administrative sciences still are more dedicated to the public sector as far as employment is concerned than on average are the other social sciences. In the 1994-6 data, tax law (100 per cent; these figures are not included in any table) and public law (87 per cent) showed above average recruitment shares into the public sector, the discipline of administrative science a below average share (64 per cent) and the other administrative sciences average figures.

What is remarkable in the disciplines of business studies, in turn, is not the high share of those gone who have gone in to work in the private business sector or the non-profit sector but the high share of those entering the public sector, namely one quarter. This is about the same share as the total share of occupationally active Finns working in the public sector – but note that the educational field in question is business studies! Among the business studies disciplines, the highest share of those recruited in the public sector was in business law (30 per cent) and the lowest in management and organisation (19 per cent), with accounting and marketing situated close to the average. It is worth mentioning that in the non-administrative social sciences social work had the high recruitment figure of 86 per cent into public sector jobs followed by social policy (79 per cent). Political science had the low figure of 54 per cent.

Table 3   Recruitment by Sector of University of Tampere Graduates of 1994-6 into Different Sectors of Employment

Field of Degree	Business	Social Scientists, non-Administrative Scientists	Social Scientists, Administrative Scientists
Sector	Per cent		
Private sector: business, voluntary association, or other	71	30	19
Public sector: national government, municipality, national churches, public enterprises	25	64	77
Other	4	6	4
Total	100	100	100

A consideration of changes in the sectoral recruitment pattern in 1994-6 sheds more light on the orientation of the three disciplinary groups. No systematic changes are visible in the pattern of the non-administrative social sciences. The administrative sciences, in turn, seem to have been turning slowly away from the public sector towards employment in the private sector. However, the surprising result is that the business graduates of 1994-96 were turning away from employment in the private sector towards finding jobs in the public sector. The change is actually very considerable, from 17 per cent of graduates of 1994 up to 37 per cent of those of 1996. What is more, it is the public sector that has been shrinking due to such reasons as privatisation of government companies, which would not lead one to expect a high willingness of public organisations to engage in recruitment (Table 4).

There are several possible reasons for the observable changes in the emphasis of recruitment. One possible reason is that businesses have remained extremely recruitment-averse, which has forced business graduates to seek employment in the public sector. Another reason is that the principles of operation in public organisations have changed towards those of business. In point of fact, in 1994-6 there was still only one discipline in the administrative sciences, namely financial administration and public sector accounting, which had been designed to meet the new challenges brought about by changes in the public sector. The output of that discipline, with only very meagre resources until 1997, could in no way satisfy the demand. We can also connect these findings to the combination of high employment and rather high recruitment beyond the public sector in the venerable core discipline of Public Administration, namely the discipline of administrative science. It is possible that the changes in public sector jobs have forced graduates in that discipline to seek employment increasingly in the private sector, if anywhere This, in turn, has pushed them into direct competition with certain graduates from business studies (in particular management and organisation) and also political science.

Table 4   Employment by Sector of University of Tampere Graduates of 1994-6 by Certain Disciplinary Fields

Field of Degree	Business			Non-Administrative Social Sciences			Administrative Sciences		
Sector of Employment	1994	1995	1996	1994	1995	1996	1994	1995	1996
	Per cent								
Private: business or non-profit	77	74	61	26	35	29	13	20	22
Public sector incl. Public enterprises	17	22	37	69	63	61	80	78	73
Other	6	4	2	5	2	10	7	2	5
Total	100	100	100	100	100	100	100	100	100
N	52	54	55	102	118	129	30	45	45

In-Service Training and Staff Development in Finnish Public Administration

Institutional Providers and Type of Training; Post-Entry Pre-Service Training

During the entire period of Finland's independence post-entry pre-service training in the field of Public Administration and all closely related fields has been absent rather than present. Only outside the civilian public sector in the army has a dedicated training system existed (and continues to exist). Traditionally, the career officer's basic multi-year education has been seen as an equivalent to a Bachelors degree, although a dedicated path up to and including doctorates in military disciplines was opened only at the turn of the 1980s and the 1990s.

The few other remaining traces of post-entry pre-service training include the police, where traditionally a two-tier training system has existed, made up of a Police School and a Police College. However, unlike military training, until the late 1990s the system was not academic at all. Only in

1998 has the education of experienced police officers with the basic lower police chief training started towards a Masters degree to qualify them for the highest police chief positions. Until the introduction of those degrees, the typical training of the senior police chiefs has been a university degree in law. It is relevant that the new training takes place as training for a Masters in Administrative Sciences with the major in administrative science, subfield security (police) administration or subfield criminology. These new arrangements make part of an overall upgrading, which has also brought into existence a new Police Polytechnic for sub-university police training. As Finland's only polytechnic in this sense so far, the degree awarded is accepted as a direct equivalent to a Bachelors degree, enabling access to university studies in the same field.

In-Service Training

A key characteristic of in-service civil service training in Finland has been the relative absence of centralised solutions both on the national and the municipal level. On the former level, a fairly systematic effort was made between the 1960s and the 1980s to coordinate in-service training through the Office for Training at the Ministry of Finance and also by means of the Government Training Centre established in the mid-1960s. Note that that establishment happened to coincide with the foundation of the academic administrative sciences in the country, first at the University of Tampere in 1965.

Even after the consolidation in the mid-1960s, a considerable part of in-service training continued to be organised by the individual ministries and agencies themselves. As far as the Government Training Centre organised courses, participation in these was typically voluntary, and ministries assigned their personnel to them depending on their own assessment of training needs instead of being bound by centralised government norms. Accountants and auditors were de facto sent to courses in government accounting and auditing, budget officials to training in budgeting, secretaries for the upgrading of secretarial skills, and so on. The Office for Training remained only a coordinator instead of a strong regulatory body.

In the municipal sector, the former two leading associations of municipalities, one for the urban and the other for the rural municipalities,

both had their training centres. Again, the centres provided training for civil servants who their host municipalities wished to assign to the courses.

Between the late 1980s and 1998 the Finnish civil service training that existed was by and large disbanded or its nature was crucially transformed. The Government Training Centre has become a consulting public corporation which provides training only as a minor part of its functions and strictly on the basis of full cost recovery and an intention to generate a surplus. The Office for Training at the Ministry of Finance has been closed, although some of its previous functions have been moved to the Ministry's Department of Personnel. One of the municipal training centres has been closed and the other has been turned into the company *Efektia*, which sells services to municipalities and other domestic and international customers on a full cost recovery basis and with a profit motive. The deep economic depression of 1992-6 also generally greatly decreased demand for and supply of civil service training.

A special field of civil service training that has continued to be nurtured in Finland is leadership training. Management and leadership courses have been and continue to be organised at the former Government Training Centre, now the Finnish Public Management Institute. However, the Institute has to compete with the universities' extension studies centres and other providers including commercial private-sector bodies. The innovation-promoting quasi-non governmental organisation *SITRA* has a coordinating role in the organisation of training in economic policy-making for leading civil servants and politicians. The courses in defence policy-making also bear a certain resemblance to civil service training for the top echelons. This concerns, in particular, the long, intensive courses for carefully selected élite participants invited both from the public and private sectors. It is the élite members who are supposed to know each other and also their functions should a serious military crisis expose Finland to an imminent threat.

Since the turn of the 1980s and 1990s there has been a trend towards awarding special diplomas of competence for certain civil servants and other participants who complete courses for upgrading their competences. The former Government Training Centre organised some such courses, and so have the universities' extension studies centres.

The universities' extension studies centres provide open university courses, short courses aiming at upgrading of selected competences, and long courses aiming at upgrading the participants' specialist skills.

Examples of civil service training worth mentioning include many short and long courses for health care and social welfare managers, school administators and headmasters and such specialists as those who aim at completing the unique Finnish official examination of national and local government auditors (JHTT).

An example of a remarkable special civil service training effort is made up of preparing civil servants for Finland's chairmanship in the European Council of Ministers for the second half of 1999. A government allocation of 40 M FIM (ca 7 MECU) was earmarked for the purpose. The number of trainees has risen to a few thousand, although the intensity of the training varied by participant, need and sector.

Conclusions

An Internationally Unique Sector of Administrative Sciences in Finland

The Finnish national government enabled the establishment of a massive sector of administrative sciences between the mid-1960s and the early 1990s. The fastest expansion took place between the end of the 1970s and the end of the 1980s. During that period the establishment of all permanent teaching positions and the filling of full professors' positions were still tightly controlled by the Ministry of Education. However, it was usually the universities themselves which had to use their initiative to apply for the establishment of positions, although it was for the Ministry of Education together with the Ministry of Finance and the various parliamentary committees to accept or reject the proposals.

The ultimate result was that administrative sciences are now present at seven of Finland's ten full-scale universities. Of the three remaining universities, the University of Turku does de facto pursue administrative research in its Department of Political Science, although it phased out its orientation in Administrative Studies at the turn of the 1980s and 1990s. Turku also cooperates with Public Administration at the Åbo Akademi university in the same town. The Universities of Jyväskylä and Oulu offer no administrative sciences at all. At Jyväskylä several other social sciences are well represented, but Oulu's conscious choice has been not to develop strong social sciences at all but to concentrate upon such fields as high-

technology electronics and medicine. There are also other university level institutions in Finland beside the universities, name y the Business Schools and the Universities of Technology, but in none of them have administrative sciences been established. The most determined effort to this end involved the aims at the Helsinki School of Economics and Business Administration to establish a dedicated programme in public sector accounting.

Implications of the Absence of a Public Sector Career System in Finland

During the entire period of Finland's independence of eighty years, a general critical attitude towards civil service and civil servants has prevailed among politicians and citizens. Leading civil servants used to have a safe tenure and even now have retained some security of employment. They also possess *de facto* power, although the political control over them has been generally strengthened. It has become easier to lay off civil servants especially at the top. Municipalities have used their opportunities to remove their city managers quite extensively. This hits administrative sciences hard, as very many city managers have had an education in this field.

The national and the municipal civil service does have legitimacy due to the numerous services it renders in such important fields as health care, education and social welfare, which employ the bulk of the civil servants. Citizens typically feel that the public sector and the civil service are excessively large, but they complain vociferously whenever a cutback has an impact upon the services they themselves demand. The military and the police enjoy a generally high legitimacy among the citizens. This concerns, in particular, those citizens who have become concerned about the slowly increasing inflow of foreigners to Finland.

A Finnish peculiarity of the 1960s and the 1970s, in particular, was a widespread politicisation of the civil service. This meant typically the observation of the political affiliation of candidates to civil service positions at the nomination stage. This practice was probably part of the price of the anti-élitist aspirations denying Finland any strict career system in her civil service. The national ministries and the municipalities were typical fields of the Finnish version of the internationally ill-fated *spoils system*. Candidates who unexpectedly lost a competition for a position to younger and less experienced but better politically affiliated candidates were generally embittered. Public opinion condemned the practice and the consequent

division of many positions and also certain public organisations or parts thereof between the political parties which held most of the cabinet seats.

At the same time as the expansion of the civil service stopped at the end of the 1980s, politicisation started generally to decline. It is relevant that as a tedious procedure of expert assessments used to be crucial at the nominations to the universities' professorial positions, there was hardly any trace of the spoils system in academia. Now that the procedure has been deregulated, some features of the spoils system may appear, as the universities are no longer prevented from promoting their internal favourites within the broad boundaries of law.

Finland is not unlike Sweden nor the other Scandinavian countries in that administrative sciences and their equivalents enjoy no special privileges as regards the entry of their graduates into the civil service. However, the de facto entry of the graduates is part and parcel of the very raison d'être of the administrative sciences.

The absence of a career system in any narrow sense in the Finnish national and municipal governments means that the administrative sciences have since their inception been in a somewhat awkward position. This is so although their de facto success in having their graduates employed has been better than in the social sciences in general. Despite the economic depression of 1992-6 and the still continuing and perhaps again increasing government cutbacks the employment record of administrative sciences graduates is at least satisfactory. In some disciplines it is good, and in some of them the degree output is still clearly too small to prevent the recruitment of graduates of business studies into the public sector instead of administrative scientists.

The Finnish national and municipal governments find themselves in an awkward position regarding the development of the civil service. On the one hand, Finland has followed the general trend of equalising terms of employment between the public and the private sectors, such as raising the minimum retirement age in the public sector, lowering the public sector pensions, making lay-offs of civil servants increasingly easy, and also implementing lay-offs including managerial and expert personnel. Public opinion in Finland is hostile towards substantial salaries and other benefits paid to civil servants. On the other hand, there are fields where public sector salaries are not attractive and Public Administration is therefore threatened by the departure of talent. Although in principle it has been made possible for public organisations to engage in free contracting on salaries and other benefits with their managers and specialists, the tight fiscal situation has generally ruled this out. At most, available resources have been exploited for pay rises to selected top managers and experts.

Extreme Differentiation and Decisive Separation from Political Science in the Finnish Administrative Sciences

The Finnish administrative sciences show evidence of an extreme and continously advancing differentiation. There is a very high and ever increasing number of teaching disciplines. There are also specialisations within disciplines and also to a limited extent between disciplines. This suggests that these disciplines have ended up reacting to the needs of the labour markets by trying to tailor ever new specialisms to appeal to representatives of important labour market niches, especially in the public sector, and especially as where demand has not yet been satisfied.

For the major part the Finnish administrative sciences are still what they are through the administrative definitions of the Ministry of Education. There continues to be government statutory regulation as to which disciplines belong within the administrative sciences, which of these disciplines are acceptable major disciplines in academic degrees, and which universities may award the degrees. Among the Finnish adminstrative sciences, it is only the discipline of administrative science which could have autonomy as a social science.

Where the discipline of administrative science could be the most independent and lead over the other disciplines, namely at the University of Tampere, the domain of the discipline is split into four independent disciplines divided into two different departments, each of which are independent result units of the university. In Tampere the administrative sciences which have received nationwide recognition as top teaching disciplines also lie outside the core Public Administration and governance area, namely public law and regional studies and environmental policy. Nor has the Tampere discipline of administrative science been a source of recent recruitments to the other administrative sciences even at the same university, but rather the reverse has come to be the case.

At the second largest Finnish concentration of administrative sciences after Tampere, i.e., at the University of Vaasa, on the contrary, unity has been maintained in the discipline of administrative science. That discipline had a predominant position vis-à-vis the other administrative sciences until the ultimate establishment of several departments in 1998. A certain extreme in maintaining disciplinary unity in the present field is administrative studies at the University of Helsinki, which has never been separated into more than one of the orientations within the teaching discipline of political science. This unity has also lately turned out to be a strength.

References

Ahonen, P. (1994), 'Political Economy: A Perspective of Finnish Research on Policy, Public Administration and Politics' in P. Ahonen, (ed.) *Political Economy of Finnish Public Administration, pp. 74-157.* Finnpublishers, Tampere.

Ahonen, P and Salminen, A. (1997), *Metamorphosis of the Administrative Welfare State: Theory and Evaluation.* Peter Lang, Frankfurt.

Mälkiä, M., Nalli, S. and Tuominen, P. (1997*),* 'Pojat vievät parhaat paikat: Hallintotieteiden maisterien työhönsijoittumiseen vaikuttavat tekijät', *Hallinnon Tutkimus,* vol. 16, 2 pp. 129-152.

OPM (1994), *Kadonnutta imperiumia etsimässä: Hallintotieteiden koulutusalan arviointi.* Ministry of Education, Helsinki.

Temmes, M. and Salminen, A. (1994), 'The Evolution of Public Administration and Administrative Research in Finland: An Historical Overview' in Modeen, T. (ed), *Public Administration in Finland,* pp. 7-25. Finnish Branch of the International Institute of Administrative Sciences. Helsinki.

Temmes, M. (1997), *Eurooppalaiset hallinnot.* VM HKO, Helsinki

University of Tampere, (1998), Results of a Survey on Graduates of the University of 1996, mimeo.

Annex 1 Finnish University Education in Public Administration, 1997-1998

University	Result unit	Discipline	Professors	Highest Degree	Year Started
Tampere	Dept. of Administrative Science	Administrative Science (1965-94 Public Administration)	2	Dr Adm. Sci.	1965
		Administrative Science, orientation in Security (Police) Administration	1 (1998-2003)	Dr. Adm. Sci.	1998
		Administrative Science, orientation in Criminology	1 (1998-2003)	Dr. Adm. Sci.	1998
		Financial Management and Public Sector Accounting	2	Dr. Adm. Sci.	1992
	Dept. of Local Government Studies	Municipal Politics	2	Dr. Adm. Sci.	1965
		Municipal Economics	2	Dr. Adm. Sci	1994
		Municipal Law	1	B. Adm. Sci.	-
	Dept. of Public Law	Public Law	3	Dr. Adm. Sci.	1965
		Tax Law	1	Dr. Adm. Sci.	1995
	Dept. of Regional Studies and Environmental Policy	Regional Studies	3	Dr. Adm. Sci.	1965
		Environmental Policy	1	Dr. Adm. Sci.	1994
Åbo Akademi University	Dept. Public Administration	Public Administration	1	Dr. Social Science (Dr. of Politics)	1980
Vaasa	Dept. of Public Management	Administrative Science (till 1994 Public Administration)	2	Dr. Adm. Sci.	1983
		International Administration	1 (temporary)	Not known yet	1998
	Dept of Public Law	Public Law	1	Dr. Adm. Sci.	1983
	Dept. Of Social and Welfare Administration and Economic Sociology	Social and Welfare Administration	1	Dr. Adm. Sci.	1995
		Economic Sociology	1	Dr. Adm. Sci.	..
	Outside departments	Regional Studies		Dr. Adm. Sci	1988

Kuopio	Dept. of Health Care Administration and Health Economics	Health Care Administration	2	Dr Public Health	1978
		Health Economics	1	Dr. Public Health	1994
	Faculty of Social Sciences	Public Law	1	Minor field	-
Helsinki	Dept. of Political Science	Political Science, orientation in Administrative Studies	3	Dr. Social Science	1963
	Swedish Social and Municipal College	Public Administration (Political Science with Municipal Administration)	1	B. Social Science, continuation to M. and Dr. in Political Science	..
		Municipal Economics and Accounting	..		..
Lapland	Faculty of Social Sciences	Administrative Science (till 1994 Public Administration)	1	Dr. Adm. Sci.	1986
		Public Law	1	Dr. Adm. Sci	1982
Joensuu	Faculty of Social Sciences	Public Law	1 (plus one in tax law[1])	M. Adm. Sci., Dr. foreseen	1997
At 7 of Finland's 10 full-scale universities	Twelve	13 at doctoral level plus 3-4 at subdoctoral level plus two orientations within one of the disciplines	37	-	-

[1] Not included in the end of column sum.

Annex 2 Examples of Finnish University Curricula Related to Public Administration

1. University of Tampere

1.1. Masters Degree in Administrative Sciences in the Teaching Discipline of Administrative Science (1965-94 Public Administration) 160 study weeks (credit units)/320 ECTS (European Credit Transfer system units)

General Studies 20/40
Basic Studies 15/30
*   Theory and Scope of Administrative Science 3/6
*   Organisation Theory and Management 3/6
*   Research Methods 2/4
*   Public Administration in Finland EU 4/8
*   Public Administration in the European Union and Its Member States 3/6
Major Field Studies 35/70
*   Strategic Thinking, Decision-Making and Management 3/6
*   Public Information Systems 2/4
*   Organisation Analysis and Design 3/6
*   Human Resources Management 2/4
*   Work Communities and Their Development 2/4
*   Leadership in Organisations 2/4
*   Survey Research 3/6
*   Organisational Assessment 4/8
*   Inception Seminars to Research Work 6/12
*   Bachelors Seminar and Thesis 8/16
Advanced Studies 40/80
*   Public Services and Their Organisation 4/8
*   Individual, Organisation and Society 4/8
*   Management and Evaluation of Change in Public Administration 3/6
*   Europe and the Globalisation Process, 3/6
*   Research on Organisation and Management 6/12
*   Seminar and Masters Thesis 20/40
Compulsory and Elective Minor Studies 50/100

1.2. Masters Degree in Administrative Sciences in the Teaching Discipline of Financial Management and Public Sector Accounting 160 study weeks/320 ECTS

General Studies 20/40
Basic Studies 15/30
*   Introduction to the Business Organisation 1/2
*   Financial Management and Policy in Europe and Finland 1/2

- Introduction to Business Accounting 3/6
- Introduction to Public Sector Financial Management 3/6
- Public Sector Financial Accounting 3/6
- Public Sector Management Accounting 2/4
- Computer Aided Financial Management 1/2
- Introduction to Auditing and Evaluation 1/2

Major Field Studies 25/50

- Public Sector Management Accounting 3/6
- Public Sector Financing Systems 2/4
- Approaches and Methods of Evaluation 2/4
- Methods for Public Sector Financial Management 1/2
- Socioeconomic Accounting 3/6
- Performance/Value for Money Auditing and Compliance Auditing 3/6 or
- Internal Auditing and Controller Systems 2/4
- Evaluation in the European Union 2/4, lectures, seminar, exam on set books
- Thesis Studies: Preparation and Thesis 10/20

Advanced Studies 40/80

- Economic Approaches to Public Policy and Organsations 3/6
- European and Finnish Policy Analysis 2/4
- Theory of Public Sector Accounting 3/6
- Theories of Auditing 2/4
- Economic and Financial Questions of Europe 4/8
- Consultative and Qualitative Evaluation 3/6
- Independent Research Including Masters Thesis 23/46

Compulsory and Elective Minor Studies 60/120

2. University of Vaasa

Masters Degree in Administrative Sciences in the Teaching Discipline of Administrative Science 160 study weeks/320 ECTS

General Studies 20/40
Basic Studies 15/30

- Introduction to Administrative Science 3/6
- Public Management Systems 3/6
- Welfare Policies and the Economy 3/6
- Research Methods 3/6
- International Administration 3/6

Major Field Studies 25-33/50-66

- Bachelors Seminar and Thesis 6/12
- Comparative Local and Regional Government 4/8
- Public Services in European Welfare States 4/6
- Governance in the European Union 3/6

- Research Methods II
- Management in Public Organisations 3/6
- Budgeting, Accounting and Auditing 4/8

Elective Major Field Studies:
- Qualitative Comparative Analysis 2/4
- Finnish Environmental Policy in the International Context 3/6

Advanced Studies 45/90
- Comparative Analysis on European Governments and Administration 3/6
- Internship 3/6 (provided as part of the the general studies at other universities offering administrative sciences in Finland)
- Research Methods III
- International Policy Making 3/6
- Evaluation of Service Organisations 3/6
- Entrepreneurship in the Public Sector 3/6
- Research Seminar and Masters Thesis 25/50

Compulsory and Elective Minor Studies 47-55/94-110.

3 The Revered Tradition: Public Administration Education and Training in France

HÉLÈNE GADRIOT-RENARD

Introduction

Education and training in Public Administration reflect the place and importance given to the Civil Service in a country, although it has to take present-day realities into account national practice in this sphere undoubtedly has its roots in history. So as to fully understand the idiosyncrasies of the French system of education and training in Public Administration it is therefore necessary to briefly consider the conditions and circumstances which have given birth to the present French context in this particular field.

The Civil Service has held an extremely important position in France for a long time, not only in terms of staff numbers, but also in the role granted to it by the public powers. It is supposed to ensure the effectiveness and continuity of decisions which it makes and this was already the case well before the Revolution of 1789. In fact, one may talk about the centralisation of power and therefore of an increasing importance of the administrative arm as long back as of the reign of King Louis XIV, from 1635 to 1715. The Prime Minister of that time, Colbert, remains an emblematic figure of administrative centralisation and of the regulation of a part of the economy, which he thought was necessary for the security of the country. Colbert, for instance, planned the planting and exploiting of French forests, the timber of which was essential to the construction of the numerous ships needed to wage war against Britain and other sea powers. The Navy was so important at that time that Colbert also created a retirement scheme for sailors. There was no question of the Welfare State then of course, but the supreme interests of the country legitimated that the State should decide on these issues.

This long-standing tradition explains why the present French Civil Service in its widest sense represents approximately a sixth of the working population, that is to say about five million people, which makes it one of the most important in the European Union.

Civil Servants from the territorial communities and a large part of hospital personnel together with State civil servants are all members of the Civil Service. These members of staff have a very important role to play in extremely diversified fields affecting the life of the country, whether it is with regard to the present or to the future, which explains the importance which must be given to the training they receive.

The level of initial recruitment, and therefore training, has for a long time been the foundation of the administrative service, which is based on a career system (as opposed to a position system) in which grade is distinct from duty. But the acceleration of technical progress and globalisastion have underlined the necessity for constant adaptation of the personnel to renewed challenges. The initial training acquired when first taking up a post is then not always adequate, and the necessity for continuous training has become imperative and has, therefore, seen development in an exponential way (and with a certain degree of success). Furthermore, the objectives of modernising the Civil Service require fundamental reflection on its means, aims and organisation and research into administrative matters, which until not long ago was barely it its infancy, but has in recent years rapidly expanded.

Initial Recruitment

Initial Recruitment is based on two fundamental notions of French thinking: a strong hierarchy and a demand for equality which ranks as constitutional law. The initial recruitment of civil servants is carried out with very few exceptions through competitive examinations. They are considered the best way of avoiding nepotism while applying Article 6 of the Declaration of Human Rights[1] which ranks as constitutional law and stipulates that the law is the same for all and that all citizens being equal in the eyes of the law have a right to public rewards and jobs according to their capacity and without any other distinction than that of their virtues or talents. This system is supposed to ensure impartiality in the recruitment of civil servants, and to guarantee that it is based on competence and the respect for ethical values shared on a nation-wide scale.

It illustrates the legal and administrative tradition of the country, which was reinforced at the end of the 19th century after the industrial revolution, when the growing importance of a liberal State resulted in a significant increase in the number of civil servants. Then, the fundamental principles of French administration slowly got into shape. One of them was and remains absolute neutrality towards the political forces, the old image of an administration at the command of political powers being done with, since civil servants serve the State but not its rulers. A subsequent principle is that the Civil Service should treat all citizens equally – including of course its own workforce. Consequently, the rights and obligations of civil servants were strictly defined first through the successive decisions of the Conseil d'Etat [2] then by law in 1946, when a statutory framework was given to the Civil Service. In 1959 the different changes which had been brought to the 1946 Act over the years were incorporated in a new general statute which has itself been amended since (from 1983 to 1986).

The general statute asserts that the unquestionable criteria and the principle of equity which the French Civil Service tradition values will be respected. Consequently, recruitment in the Service has to follow the very rules which will later determine the position of recruits inside the Service.

It is important to understand that people thus recruited to the Civil Service have reached a certain level of education. The statute of the Civil Service provides for three categories of staff, A, B, and C, which correspond to different levels of recruitment and of course to different levels of job responsibility. The preparation of competitive exams does not really take on a definite form at C, which is the lowest, and the civil servants recruited at this level do not generally follow a training course after recruitment. The competitive exam at this level is essentially used as a means of ensuring objectivity in recruitment. But it involves much more with regards to categories B and A. The competitive exam giving access to the former is of an undergraduate level, while graduates and postgraduates compete for positions in the A category. The actual preparation is essentially (but not obligatorily) carried out within the Institutes of Political Sciences (which have a private status) or, but more marginally in the universities. Incidentally, and strange as it may seem, universities have not really developed their own types of administrative training; some classes about Public Administration or administrative science are given either by law specialists or political analysts at postgraduate level, but they are more connected with research in the field of administrative science than with the down to earth preparation of exams.

Although there are some exceptions, particularly in the Foreign Service, most examinations in the A category are supposed to lead to the recruitment of versatile (as opposed to specialised) civil servants. Hence the curricula are extremely vast. The candidates must of course be conversant in public law, mainly the Constitution and law related to the civil rights and civil liberties. As there is a specific law in France for administrative matters, the jurisdictions being different too, would-be civil servants are also expected to be familiar with the contents and peculiarities of administrative law. Needless to say, they must be proficient in economics - not only theories but also practice, which means being able to understand, and sometimes build, economic models.   Programmes include public finance as well; national accounting, the principles of public accountancy, techniques in structural and performance analysis, the assessment of public policies etc. A good knowledge of international affairs is another requisite, which means not only being aware of the geostrategic issues of the time but also having a satisfactory command of international law. Labour relations and social law are also within the scope of the overall curriculum.

In general, the competitive examination is divided into two parts; the first part is a written exam, which selects the candidates with best results (representing between two and three times the number of available posts) whereas during the second part, which is oral, the final selection of candidates is made.

Passing the competitive examination opens up access to different training institutes which are in reality specialised institutes in which candidates will have to put into practice the theoretical knowledge they have acquired preparing for the competitive examination. It should be stressed that from the moment they pass the exam and enter the specialised institution, students are considered as trainee civil servants and are paid as such.

With regards to the State Civil Service, nearly fifty specialised schools – excluding teacher and military training colleges – train the trainee civil servants in the particular needs of the Ministerial departments to which they are attached. Examples include The National College for Taxation, The Customs School, The Treasury School and Police schools. Non-specialist executives of the Civil Service are trained within the five Regional Administrative Institutes (IRA), and top civil servants attend the College for Senior Civil Servants (Ecole Nationale d'Adminstration, the renowned and controversial ENA). In addition Ecole Polytechnique and engineering schools provide training for the high-ranking technical corps of the State. Most of these schools do not have any permanent teaching staff, but use senior civil servants or university professors as trainers. A significant part of the training is done in the field with senior civil servants as tutors.

Territorial civil servants are trained at the National Training Centre of the territorial Civil Service (Centre National de la Fonction Publique Territoriale – CNFPT) and Civil Service hospital personnel are trained at the National College of Public Health (Ecole Nationale de Sante Publique – ENSP) as far as administrative staff is concerned, whereas nurses attend the various Nursing Schools. The training of doctors is quite a different matter (they generally do not belong to the civil service).

The principle of competitive examination is not fundamentally questioned for it is accepted as a democratic means of access to all levels of the Civil Service. Furthermore, this system, through a process of selection, ensures an uncontestable level of competence; one candidate out of seven passes the examination for category A and one out of nine passes the exam for ENA. At the higher levels, the French Civil Service effectively attracts the best students. But there is increasing criticism about the fact that such early success in a competitive examination offers life tenure. Besides, the actual degree of social equality provided by the system is repeatedly debated, since it is obvious to all that previous training and the socio-cultural context of participants partially determine to a certain extend the possibility of access to a given level of training and thus the chances of passing the examinations.

But it is interesting to note at this point that this absolute principle – no access to the public service without passing an examination – explains the French attitude, which is prudent, if not wary and sometimes hostile to 'affirmative action' policies involving the promotion of categories of the disadvantaged population. Once it is generally accepted that the systems of school and university education theoretically provide access for all categories of the population to these forms of objective and egalitarian recruitment, it does not appear necessary, it would even seem undemocratic, to 'bend the rules' via operations which do not recognise common rules.

To this must be added the conviction of the unquestionable unity of the nation, firmly anchored in each citizen and reaffirmed in Article 1 of the 1958 Constitution; 'France shall be an indivisible, secular, democratic and social Republic. It shall ensure the equality of all citizens before the law without distinction of origin, race or religion'. The French tradition has never encouraged the persistence of communities but has on the contrary favoured the assimilation of populations of different origins in a common mould. Recent trends stressing the need for difference of treatment according to the difference of culture or gender strongly antagonise this deep-rooted tradition. This is definitely a controversial point in the country today, and has lately fuelled passionate debates, which although initiated in political life have now extended to the public service. But although the need to facilitate the access to higher education for disadvantaged students and to break down the 'glass-ceiling' blocking women from higher positions is endlessly stressed, the principle of a competitive examination giving access to positions in the civil service is not seriously criticised on these grounds. But such a formalised mechanism nevertheless attracts much heated criticism.

The contents of the programmes[3] preparing for the examinations are said to be too technical, too restricted and not open enough to the problems of the outside world. They consequently encapture the future 'technocrat' into a world which is cut off from everyday matters. Moreover, if the system of competitive examinations enables the capacity of assimilation of knowledge of the candidates to be judged, it gives absolutely no clue to their actual professional ability.

Furthermore, these means of recruitment are held responsible for the lack of flexibility of the organisation of the Civil Service. All is supposed to be decided straight after recruitment; each individual put in his or her right place, with critics emphasising the fact that the whole thing seems to enhance a 'once a sailor, always a sailor' pattern of positions in the Service. This would correspond to the strong hierarchical tradition in French public life, which impregnated social relations under the former monarchy and which the Revolution did not suppress at all. A centralised and hierarchical Civil Service enables the continuous serving of a powerful State which remains centralised in spite of a voluntary policy of decentralisation first undertaken in 1983. But this inevitably leads to self-withdrawal and insensitivity on the part of the Civil Service to external influences and concerns. Last but not least, such extreme forms of hierarchy would paralyse the desires of staff at the lower levels to take initiatives.

Whether these drawbacks should justify tearing the whole house down is a moot point. No one denies that civil servants have to be selected one way or another but if the programmes leading to the examinations are not always satisfactory, one might paraphrase Churchill's famous words about democracy by saying of the selection process that it is a bad system but that the others would be worse. More positively answers have been given, with constant improvement in mind, to remedy faults in the initial machinery.

It is undeniable that a traditional rigidity still governs most of the hierarchical relations within the French Civil Service and that it is a reflection of French society when it refuses to take 'invisible' inequalities into account, and in particular those linked to gender (an equal salary is paid for an equal job in the Civil Service, but the proportion of women in the higher grades is very low with the 'glass ceiling', as in political life, being present). But in fact, the system is, from a social point of view, relatively open. It should for example be stressed that a failed former education is not necessarily a handicap since ever increasing forms of continuous training enable staff from the lower levels to accede to higher levels. This means that, contrary to current hearsay, entrance into a particular category at the beginning of a career in no way prejudices the future of an individual. The most selective competitive examination, that of Ecole Nationale d'Administration (ENA), has since 1991 been open to people coming from the private sector and who have eight years of professional experience, which enables the field of recruitment to be widened. At the same time, special examinations open to people coming from the private sector facilitate entrance to high level positions in the Civil Service to individuals from lay society who have not necessarily gone through the high level competitive examinations.

It is also incontestable that the traditional initial public service training given in the various institutes mentioned above often leaves disciplines, which have nowadays become essential to the daily practice of civil servants, in the background. This is undoubtedly still the case with the management of human resources or communication and negotiation techniques, although things are slowly changing. However it should also be remembered that in the early eighties few curricula were concerned with computer sciences as they are now, which seems to demonstrate that change is eventually integrated into the training process. The new generations benefit from these changes, but the older ones are not excluded from them since once again gaps in initial training can be filled during a career through continuous training.

Continuous Training

Although its implementation is relatively recent, continuous training is now well developed and aims at preparing the public service for the future. Continuous training follows more or less the same patterns in the three different French Civil Services (ie State, local and hospital personnel). Continuous training as such covers two main areas; preparation for the competitive examinations and advanced in-service training. To these can be added job adaptation and training or secondment leaves; the latter being opportunities given to certain categories of civil servants – essentially teachers and army personnel – to take a paid leave varying from one to three years in order to get a new job.

On 29th June 1989 the Government and Civil Service Trade Unions drafted an outline agreement on training which stipulated that 2 per cent of the Civil Service wage bill should be devoted to continuous training (not including job adaptation and training leaves). The actual spending on continuous training now exceeds 4 per cent of the wage bill, and reaches more that 7 per cent of the wage bill when job adaptation and training leaves are included.

The most traditional form of in service training is the preparation for competitive examinations, which can have different aims, from enabling a non civil servant member of staff or a trainee to be appointed to the Civil Service to giving access to a higher category in the Service to those already belonging to it. Each ministerial service organises training programmes which are free for their staff and take place either in training institutes or schools which already offer initial training, or at the place of work. Courses are given by civil servants versed in the subject or, less frequently for reasons of costs, by outside agencies. Courses are held mostly during work time or at lunchtime and occasionally after hours. The frequency of classes (from once a week to everyday) is in direct relation to the level of the examination. Age limits for candidates vary according to the type of examination involved, but special cases (lone mothers, mothers of three and more, etc.) are given laxer limits. It was decided some years ago to level upwards and sometimes even to cancel these age limits so as to facilitate the recruitment of new people, and thus try giving a response to the various criticisms aimed at early recruitment. But the measure has posed quite a few problems – among which are identifying the crucial points of an interesting career span for the candidate beneficial for the Service – and there now are discussions about the necessity of reintroducing limits.

But the continuous training in knowledge and the consolidation of competence are also a major concern of the administrative services, anxious to reply to the criticisms aimed at beginning of career competitive recruitment. This is why the outline agreement on training of June 1989 was complemented by an agreement on continuous training signed on 22nd February 1996, which stipulated that all civil servants must be given access to a programme of training which is recorded on an individual training index card and that each administrative body must therefore draw up a global programme of forecasted training and indicate its expected influence on each individual; the whole process being drawn up in consultation with the staff and their trade union representatives.

As a result, the percentage of trained staff as compared to existing staff now exceeds 100 per cent a year – which does not mean of course that each and everyone of the civil servants goes through a training programme but that those who do follow more than one session. The ratio of training time as compared with working time is nearly 4 per cent on average (the ratio is higher - more that 7 per cent - for higher categories of staff, which can be explained by the greater difficulty of training at this level and the ensuing need to devote more time to it).

Curiously enough, in spite of these measures having been taken in order to offer fairness and to remedy gaps left after initial training, it is the lower levels of staff who are the most reticent in taking advantage of training courses (this attitude is frequently referred to as 'the return to school syndrome.') Some of them certainly have the wary attitude of former drop-outs towards whatever form of training might remind them of their school years. But they also fear that the methods of follow-up on training (programme and individual index card) may be used in ways which could be unfavourable to them, with for instance a negative impact on their career prospects if they refuse a training offer or did not do well during courses.

Intermediate managers are also often hostile, for on the one hand a member of staff committed to training is frequently absent from work, and on the other hand, successful results could lead to the staff member leaving the department hence creating a problem of replacement. The success of continuous training is therefore dependent upon measures of flexibility within the different departments. In France, at the moment, reflection on this subject is at an embryonic stage.

The role of top managers is consequently extremely important, for not only are they responsible for the dynamic nature of training courses and the implementation of facilitating measures, but they must also convince their staff (subordinates and their immediate superiors) of the usefulness and even absolute necessity of training of staff members.

But if the development of continuous training was initially directed towards the traditional needs of the Civil Service, there is no doubt now that its scope should be – and has been – widened and steadfastly aimed towards the future, both on an internal level as well as on an international one. Thanks to the numerous training sessions they can attend, civil servants are not only more competent, but also in tune with the evolution of their environment and more capable of adapting themselves to the evolution of the administrative structure of their country as well as to demands of modernisation within the Civil Service. This is essential, because it is undeniable that the Civil Service of the third millennium will have little in common with that of today.

The all-triumphant Welfare State which dominated West European countries from 1945 onwards certainly met the expectations of populations which had been traumatised by the economic crisis of 1929 and the Second World War and which expected the State to act as an arbitrator and moderator in economic and social relations.

But things have changed and nowadays the citizens of our modern and democratic countries refuse to accept an all-powerful Civil Service which seems far removed from them, and demand a Civil Service tuned to the problems and realities of lay society. They want a less costly and more efficient system with better management, and demand 'less State intervention'. For all that they generally disapprove of the slightest sign of unequal treatment between citizens and seriously doubt the capacity of a Civil Service based on patterns in the private sector to efficiently cope with the specific problems the public sector faces, in reality they probably do not want 'less State intervention' but 'improved State intervention'.

France is unquestionably used to a mighty Civil Service which, in tune with the notion of the Welfare State, ensures the respect of general interest with all citizens without distinction being protected by legislative and regulatory acts of a State whose role has gone far beyond the sovereign tradition.

But in order to satisfy these new preoccupations, considerable effort has been undertaken in the country so as to achieve real decentralisation giving actual power to local authorities, coupled with a deconcentration of central services bringing the administrative services closer to the citizens. As a result, a member of staff is sometimes required to act in a manner which is in total contradiction with what was taught to him or her at the beginning of his or her career. This is particularly true in France of financial decisions, which were normally centralised in the hands of very few people and which recent trends have tended to decentralise down to the different local services. Years of practice have then to change, and the people who were used to going through a tedious controlling process do not necessarily find it easier to adapt to the new situation than those who were at the other end of the rope and who have to give up part of their controlling power. Only well managed and well prepared forms of training can then facilitate these decisive changes which are often upsetting, and ensure a radical transformation of mentality and practice. Continuous training has therefore taken on a crucial role – that of facilitating the adaptation of civil servants to these new aspirations of the lay society, without sacrificing the criteria of competence and ethical requirements which form the basis of the French Civil Service.

It is also necessary to accelerate the modernisation of the civil service. Far from the traditional image of 'the bureaucrat', the new civil servants will have to develop an unrivalled aptitude for change, which is necessary in order to keep up with the acceleration of technical progress and the increasingly numerous challenges imposed by a society in a constant state of evolution. They will not only be required to assure the daily running of a department, but they also will have to foresee the future evolution of their missions and therefore the adjustment of their means and structures. There generally is some delay in the adaptation of training programmes to the evolution of the surrounding world. This was obviously the case with 'computer sciences' and 'communication', but now that these two subjects are being seriously tackled, new fields are opening and training modules about the various forms of management, economic forecasting and the new information technologies have to be set up.

Last but probably not least, the training of civil servants must now take into account the European dimension of the administrative action of any member state, a dimension which is already important but which will probably become essential as the construction of the Union grows in terms of depth and width. The civil servants of the 21st century will most probably be more European than national. This does not mean of course that they will belong to some big-brother like European Civil Service, but rather that they will have to think and act increasingly with the European dimension in mind, and in respect of European law. This is probably one of the most important challenges national government departments will be faced with in the years to come.

So as to open up access to its government departments to nationals of other EU member states France has modified several articles of the Statutes of the Civil Service which until then limited access to nationals. The extension is for the moment limited to those jobs in which the attributions are separate from the exercise of sovereignty or which have neither direct nor indirect participation in the carrying out of prerogatives of the public powers of the State and its Territorial Communities. Of course a good command of French is necessary, particularly when the only way to gain a definite position is a competitive examination. Needless to say that training needs are such and financial means so scarce that no in-service training programme now caters for the needs of foreigners wanting to improve or brush up their French.

But the awareness of the importance of training in European affairs has led the government to set up a Centre for European Studies in Strasbourg (Centre d'Etudes Europeenes de Strasbourg – CEES). This Centre was opened at the end of 1994 and already has a flourishing activity in the fields of both initial and continuous training. Its courses are attended by civil servants coming from all the member states of the Union, but also by those belonging to countries wishing to join the Union in the coming years. The Centre also provides training sessions to nationals from countries all over the world who simply wish to understand how the Union works and to improve their knowledge of its structures and idiosyncrasies.

The Research Dimension

All these changes can certainly not be completed without a sustained effort in training for all levels of personnel in the Civil Service. Yet training is not enough; it must be coupled with a development of theoretical reflection on the foundations of the Civil Service - its means and ways – and on its future. That means that research into administrative matters should be developed.

Such research exists in France, but it is on the one hand not very widespread, and on the other hand relatively diluted. For a long time it was not deemed essential and took second place after administrative law and political sciences, but it has nevertheless developed thanks to the expansion of organisational sciences. But ever since the 1960s it has been split between three different trends: the legal approach, the managerial approach (represented by the contributors to the journal *Politics and Public Management)* and the sociological approach (itself divided between the supporters of the systemical approach like Gremion or Thoenig and the culturalists like Crozier).

Until recently, French universities had not developed courses in Public Administration, except at a doctoral level, and comparative research was still in its infancy. In the last few years, however, the analysis of public policy has aroused a renewed interest in research into the civil services. But it is carried out mainly by law faculties, and to a lesser extent by political scientists in the Institutes for Political Studies (Instituts d'Etudes Politiques - IEP) – particularly those in Bordeaux and Grenoble – and by sociologists working for research centres such as the National Centre for Scientific Research (Centre National de la Recherche Scientifique – CNRS).

Few of the numerous administrative schools and institutes are actually involved in that research area, with the notable exception of ENA and more specifically the International Institute for Public Administration (IIAP), which are its prime movers. The IIAP is specialised in the training of foreign civil servants who wish to better their knowledge of the French and European administrative roles and to improve their personal know-how. The research activities of the IIAP are diversified and include the organisation of colloquia and conferences, participation in international administrative networks (such as IISA), activities in the field of administrative engineering and the training of trainers in response to invitations to tender, and publications – more specifically, the Institute publishes and circulates the *French Review of Public Administration.*

Obviously research remains the weak point of training and education in the civil service in France, which probably explains why instead of anticipating changes and preparing in time for the future, training always tries to catch up with the latest development. This is sometimes true of teaching methods, which although they have long departed from the worn out traditional forms ('the talk and chalk' lecture) tend more to keep up with the Jones's than to actually find attractive new paths.

But this is probably due to the unconscious feeling that it is not necessary to change a system which has, on the whole and until very recently, given satisfaction. Things are changing though, and the dominant view is that as far as education and training in the Civil Service are concerned there should develop a clever mix between tradition and innovation managing to make the civil servants on the one hand the guardians of the past, but definitely on the other hand the architects of the future.

Notes

1. The Declaration of Human rights dates back to 1789 but ranks as constitutional law since it is referred to in the preamble to the 1958 Constitution.
2. The Conseil d'Etat is the supreme court for the Administrative Law.
3. These contents have been briefly described earlier in the text.

References

Brown, L.N. and Garner, J.F. (1993), *French Administrative Law.* 4th edn.. Clarendon Press, Oxford.

Claisse, A. and Meininger, M.C. (1994), *Fonctions publiques en Europe.* Montchrestien. Collection 'Clefs' Paris.

Frears, J. (1983), 'The decentralisation reforms in France', *Parliamentary Affairs vol.* 36, 1.

Howarth, J. and Cerny, P.G. (1981), *Elites in France: origins, reproduction and power.* Pinter, London.

IIAP, (1996), *An Introduction to French Administration.* La documentation francaise, Paris.

Keating, M. and Hainsworth, P. (1986), *Decentralisation and Change in Contemporary France.* Gower, Aldershot.

Legendre, P. (1968), *Histoire de l'administration de 1750 a nos jours.* PUF, Paris.

Mettam, R. (1977), *Government and Society in Louis XIV's France.* Macmillan, London.

Rouban, L. (1994), *Les cadres superieurs de la fonction publique et la politique de modernisation administrative.* La documentation francaise. Paris.

Rouban, L. and Ziller, J. (1995) 'De la modernisation de l'administration a la reforme de l'Etat.' *Revue francaise d'administration publique.* Juillet-Septembre 1995, no.75.

Smith, A. (1997), 'Developments in the Academic Study of Public Administration in France.' Institut d'Etudes politiques de Bordeaux, (paper presented to the British Political Studies Association's specialist group on Public Administration, London).

Thomas, Y. (1995), *Histoire de l'administration. La Decouverte.* Collection 'Reperes', Paris.

Ziller, J. (1988), *Egalite et merite*, IEAP, Maastricht.

Ziller, J. (1993), *Administrations comparees.* Montchrestien. Paris.

4 The Market for Civil Servants: Public Administration Education and Training in The Netherlands

FRITS M. VAN DER MEER AND FRANS K.M. VAN NISPEN

Introduction

The Dutch civil service has undergone profound changes over the last two decades. Although certainly not unique in this respect reform has left its mark on the size, the organisation and the preferred mode of operation of the civil service. In this contribution we will concentrate on the aspects related to the labour market for civil servants. We intend to explore the relationship between the changes in demand for civil servants and the changes in how (future) civil servants are educated and trained for a job in government. Using the 'market' metaphor we will look at the demand for and the supply of civil servants. For reasons of limitation we will concentrate on 'higher' civil servants working in central government departments.

The 'market' for civil servants has undergone radical changes since the early 1980s. A first feature which will be examined below is the changing demand for civil servants. Great efforts have been made since this period to reduce the size of public employment. After decades characterised by an ever-expanding demand for new staff, downsizing became the buzz word in the policy making community. The success of this new policy is one aspect which we will examine. Additionally and perhaps even more important for our purpose is to examine which type of jobs have been dispensed with. As we will disclose higher civil servants have been more or less 'spared'.

This policy has resulted not only in a changed public attitude towards government employment but has also fundamentally altered the composition of central government employment. The popular policy credo was 'smaller, but better government' based around American efforts to create an entrepreneurial government that 'works better and costs less'. The connection with the New Public Management motto 'value for money' can also easily be seen. New and higher professional standards were required of both the new and existing staff. In order to improve civil service quality new emphasis was put on management development (MD) and training and education programmes. With respect to training new initiatives were taken both at pre-entry and post-entry levels in order to meet changing demand. This issue will be discussed in section 4. The conclusion will complete this survey by examining programmes in Public Administration in The Netherlands.

In order to fully understand the exact nature of these changes in the Dutch public labour market it is necessary to pay attention to the political-administrative environment (Bekke, Toonen & Perry, 1996), and it is to this to which we will now turn.

The Dutch Political-Administrative System

The Netherlands is a constitutional parliamentary democracy situated in the north-western corner of Europe. In its present form the constitutional system dates from the middle of the 19th century, 1848 to be exact. According to the constitution, The Netherlands is a monarchy. The powers of the monarch are (with a few exceptions) mainly ceremonial. The monarch is seen as a symbol of national unity and continuity. Underlying the division of powers within the Dutch state is the concept of the decentralised unitary state. Although sovereignty resides in the undivided 'state' the powers of the state are divided between central, provincial and local government. Intergovernmental relations cannot be understood solely in terms of hierarchy but by emphasizing intergovernmental cooperation and adjustment. The same is true with respect to the division of powers within a particular level of government. The model operating in central government with respect to legislation is one of cooperation between the chambers of parliament and the cabinet of the day. Although cabinet is accountable to parliament and needs the explicit or implicit support of a majority, the close relations between ministers and coalition parties causes in practice an osmosis between the legislature and the executive.

No single party has ever held a majority in Parliament in modern times. Consequently, cohesive powers in central government have always been weak

(Van der Meer, Dijkstra and Roborgh, 1997), the coalition nature of Dutch government inhibiting (strong) central political direction (Van der Meer & Raadschelders, 1997). Although a cabinet structure has developed over the years, ministers (and their departments) have a large degree of autonomy. For instance the minister responsible for co-ordinating central government personnel policies (Home Affairs) cannot override another minister using his 'formal' powers in this particular field.

The fragmentation of the political landscape mirrors cleavages in Dutch society, leading to a dispersal of power and tasks and to a tradition of bargaining. Co-ordination is achieved more by negotiation and bargaining than by issuing formal directions. This tradition of bargaining is essential to an understanding of decision making in Dutch society and government. It is also to be found in social-economic relations. Whether actually as successful as is often heralded the Dutch economic 'poldermodel' is another expression of this feature of Dutch society.[1]

Because of the decentralised political administrative system, central government, provinces, and municipalities are responsible for regulating the legal position of staff employed by their organisations. A civil service act (Civil Servants Act 1929) is in force but operates as a general framework.[2] Its main purpose is to ensure that (decentralised) statutes are operative (Van der Meer, Dijkstra and Roborgh, 1997). Human resource management decisions are equally the sole responsibility of each unit of government.

Due to the absence of a strong cabinet structure most management and personnel policies are decentralised to the individual ministries. A department is responsible for hiring new staff, making career decisions, developing and running management development programmes and training policies, although an exception must be made for collective wage bargaining. To a certain extent each department can therefore be seen as an independent employer. Recently some limitations to this departmental autonomy have been introduced with respect to the higher and top civil servants. For the top civil servants at the national level the *Algemene Bestuursdienst* (ABD) has been introduced. The ABD is the Dutch equivalent of the senior executive service. It serves as a unified top executive in order to offset compartmentalisation by promoting (interdepartmental) mobility and developing management development programmes for the staff involved.

The demand for civil servants has a qualitative as well as a quantitative component that reflects the 'smaller, but better' credo. We will start by discussing the latter as operationalised in a decade of personnel reductions. We will then switch to the efforts to improve performance of the civil service by management development.

Quantitative: Efficiency Movement

In our introduction we pointed to change in policy regarding the size of the civil service dating from the early 1980s. At that particular time government launched a large-scale effort to reduce the budget deficit by targeted spending cuts. In addition, several other change processes were triggered. The government established six so-called 'major operations' to improve its performance (Van Nispen and Noordhoek, 1986). One of these was deliberately focused on the reduction of the number of central government employees by 2 per cent per year, over a four year period (1981-1985). The results of the so-called '4 x 2 per cent operation' were disappointing and the Dutch government decided stronger medicine was needed. The 4 x 2-per cent operation was replaced by a 'weight watchers'operation (1986-1990), the outcome of which was somewhat ambiguous.

The target of a personnel reduction of 25,000 employees was not met completely, but the foreseen growth in the number of employees was brought to a halt. A continuation of the efforts was deemed necessary, but the application of across-the-board cuts was no longer considered appropriate. A target of 6,000 full time equivalent posts to be shed by 1995 was set, which on paper was met. However, because of changing definitions used in compiling government statistics the precise position is unclear. Moreover, over the period in question, there have been personnel increases in policy areas not affected by operation efficiency, and these may conceal the true level of goal attainment.[3] Against this, in the early 1990s efforts to reduce the government workforce merged with those to transfer public services to the private sector in an attempt to improve efficiency.

Table 1 Number of Employees per Ministry (1995)

Ministry	FY 1995	Core	Peripheral
MP's Office	296	185	111
Foreign Office	3.636	1.090	2546
Justice	24.850	805	24045
Home Affairs	1.470	1.010	460
Education, Culture & Science	2.072	895	1177
Finance	29.760	1.000	28760
Defence[1]	103.875	875	103000
Housing, Spatial Planning & Environmental Affairs	3.850	1.400	2450
Transport & Public Works	10.635	1.600	9035
Economic Affairs	4.838	1.060	3778
Agriculture & Fishery	3.100	920	2180
Social Affairs & Employment	2.400	1.120	1280
Health Care, Sports & Welfare	4.075	945	3130
Total	194.857	12.905	181.952

1. The number of employees includes the military service.

Source: Wiegel 1993.

Table 1 shows the numbers of employees per ministry in 1995. While some of the cuts claimed through downsizing have been essentially cosmetic - for example, by changing definitions and creative accounting - and in other cases merely reflect the transfer of non-core departmental business to executive agencies, the 'market' for civil servants has become tighter with few new personnel now being employed other than in specific categories such as computer experts. Inevitably, this has had an impact on the demand for government-oriented studies like Public Administration. At the same time it should be noted that the number of *higher* civil servants has risen as a ratio of the total number of civil servants (see Table 2).[4] Thus it would appear that the market for higher civil servants is still expanding and that the brunt of the cuts have been realised in the lower echelons of the civil service.

Table 2   The Number of Higher Civil Servants as Ratio of the Total Number of Civil Servants at the National Level 1976-1994 (x 1000)

Year	Civil Servants		Percentage
	Total	High	
1976	135.1	16.6	12.3
1980	146.4	20.1	13.7
1985	154.4	24.1	15.6
1990	148.5	31.2	21.0
1994	142.4	34.7	24.1

Source: Kerngegevens bezoldiging overheidspersoneel 1976-1995.

Qualitative: Management Development

In our introduction to civil service reform we observed that civil service reform policy was not limited to cutback policies. Besides the quantitative dimension considerable attention was focused on the qualitative aspects of the civil service. While reform was brought about in part by the need to reduce the financial problems of central government, it was also realised that the role of central government in the economy and society had to be altered and that a greater contribution could be made by private organisations and groups as an alternative to direct government intervention. This, in turn, was seen to require a modernised civil service with new attributes. In particular it was required to become less bureaucratic and ready to take a more proactive posture. This aspiration was to have important consequences for personnel management with the result that since the 1980s new efforts have been made to develop active human resource policies. Crucial to these human resource policies have been management development (MD) schemes designed to develop the personal qualities and skills of higher civil servants in order to meet the demands of adequate task performance (Home Affairs, 1992). It has involved a systematic approach to the career development of higher civil servants - especially those officials who have shown particular promise - and the organisation of relevant training facilities. The particular aims of this MD policy in The Netherlands are to:

- enhance mobility within government ministries;
- to adapt to present and future function and management requirements;
- realise a better cooperation within administration;
- spread an aspired organisational culture;
- develop a reliable system of manning crucial posts (Home Affairs 1992).

It is important to observe that there is no overall MD (and training) system for the whole of central government. For the majority of (higher) personnel each department has developed its own policy. The only exception is the ABD. Usually departmental MD policies are designed under the auspices of an MD council in which the most senior departmental officials (Secretary-General, directors-general, personnel management directors) are involved. With the exception of top officials belonging to the ABD, participation in MD programmes is not compulsory, although refusal to participate may have future career implications.

Recently, attention in MD policy has been focused upon the enhancement of what is now termed 'the employability' of civil servants. One aspect of this is that a civil servant is encouraged to identify with government and the public sector in general, rather than with a particular department or unit. The main aim of this policy is to increase the flexibility of staff, promote mobility and combat compartmentalisation. This employability policy consists of three components (Home Affairs, 1997):

- The stimulation of mobility within central government
- An extensive training policy.
- An active labour market policy.

Having discussed the context of management development it is obvious that training for the civil service is a crucial element of MD policies. In the next section we will turn to the organisation and content of training for the civil service in The Netherlands.

The Supply Side of the Market

In discussing the supply side of the market for civil servants it is important to make a distinction between pre- and post-entry education and training. [5]

Pre-Entry Training

Pre-entry education is quite important due to the Dutch system of civil service recruitment. Most higher civil servants are (still) recruited under the so-called job-system, whereby an individual is recruited to a particular job. In the majority of cases the individuals concerned remain in the civil service for the rest of their working life. However, there is hardly any 'formal' policy towards career management.

The emphasis on recruitment for a particular position makes the quality and nature of pre-entry training very important. A person should be able to perform the given task almost from the start. Examining the educational background of higher civil servants employed by Dutch central government it becomes apparent that primarily those individuals are recruited with an academic or higher professional education in disciplines such as economics, law, social and technical sciences (Van der Meer and Roborgh, 1993; Van Braam, 1957).

The importance of institutions of higher education goes further than just providing pre-entry education to aspiring civil servants as these institutions also provide post-graduate courses relevant to civil servants. A university training is considered imperative for a higher civil servant and most universities are very active (for reasons of additional revenue amongst others) in this field. In 1995 the departments of Public Administration of the universities of Leiden and Rotterdam started evening classes for civil servants and a number of other universities have developed similar initiatives. One should also not neglect the use of standard university (normally, masters) courses taken by civil servants aspiring to make a career step. Universities and university staff are also often involved in post-entry courses.

Concerning disciplinary background a relative shift has occurred from the recruitment of legal trainees to the increasing employment of graduates in economics, Public Administration, political science, and technical science (Van der Meer and Roborgh, 1993). In many university (and higher professional) curricula special provisions (streams) are made for students who aim for a career or position in government. The creation of a Masters programme in Public Administration in the 1980s and specialisation in disciplines relevant to Public Administration, for instance, in law and economics are examples of how the (personnel) demands and programmes offered by higher education institutions are connected.

A look at the supply side of the market for pre-entry training in Public Administration from a historical perspective reveals that the study of Public Administration has its roots in the law school. It originally focused on the administration of local government widening afterwards to other sectors of government. It is more or less accepted that G.A.van Poelje was the 'founding father' of the study of Public Administration in The Netherlands in the early 20th century. He saw the necessity for the professionalisation of (local) civil servants having started his career as a lawyer in local government. In the late 1920s he assumed the first chair in Public Administration at the Nederlandse Economische Hogeschool, the predecessor of the Erasmus University of Rotterdam. The focus at that time was mainly on local government..

In the mid-1960s the study of Public Administration became part of the domain of political science. It started to flourish at various places as a specialism - Amsterdam, Leiden, Nijmegen - followed by the first full-fledged masters programme in Public Administration at the then Technische University of Twente at Enschede (1976). [6] A decade or so later a joint programme in Public Administration was launched by the Leiden University and the Erasmus University of Rotterdam (1984), supported by the director-general of Higher Education, a former professor of Public Administration at the Catholic University Nijmegen.[7] Later other universities followed.[8] The most recent is the University of Technology at Delft which offers a programme in Public Administration from a technological perspective. [9]

The development of the study of Public Administration as a separate discipline has been fostered by the establishment of the *Vereniging voor Bestuurskunde* (Association of Public Administration) that performs as a platform for scholars and practitioners. It issues a journal, *Bestuurskunde* (Public Administration), which is published eight times per year.

The question may be raised, 'what is Public Administration in The Netherlands about?' We are concerned here essentially with Public Administration as a discipline that prepares students for   positions in Public Administration as a profession (Waldo, 1955; Rutgers, 1993). It is more or less accepted that the study of Public Administration tries to bridge at least two gaps. Firstly, the study of Public Administration is deliberately not only descriptive, but also prescriptive in nature. One of the aims of the study of Public Administration is to improve performance in the public sector. Secondly, the study of Public Administration claims to be inter-disciplinary or at least multi-disciplinary, because problems in society do not stop at the borders of traditional disciplines (Van Braam, 1988; Hakvoort, 1989).

The last few years have featured a shift in the subject of the study of Public Administration. The procedures and organisation of the government were long seen as being at the heart of the study of Public Administration. Nowadays, however, governance is considered more and more to be the core of the discipline. Moreover, governance is no longer restricted to the public sector. The dividing line between the public and private sectors is not clearcut and is continuously changing. In line with this development is the attention that is now given to public-private partnerships.

One useful indicator of the scope of the programmes in Public Administration is the number of professors (see Table 3). Another is student enrolment in the five main programmes which showed a peak in the late 1980s. Since then the number of students has declined gradually and stabilised somewhere between 100 and 150 students per university, part-time students excluded. In addition, a smaller number of students take a Public Administration specialism as part of their study in other disciplines, mainly law and political science. The various universities not only compete for students, but also work together in areas such as the education of PhD students and exchange programmes with foreign partners. Finally, the University of Utrecht has established a Center for Policy and Management that offers a wide variety of graduate as well as postgraduate programmes.

**Table 3   The number of professors of Public Administration in
The Netherlands (1997)**

	Full Professors	Associate Professors	Assistant Professors	Total	Fte's
EUR	6	5	14	25	22.4
KUB	2	2	6	10	9.7
KUN	3	2	3	8	6.8
OU	1			1	1.0
RUL	3	4	15	22	20.9
UT[1]	9	9	20	38	34.7
Total	24	22	58	04	95.5

1. Two vacancies excluded.

Source: Visitatierapport 1998 .

A survey among graduates of the University of Twente shows that 31.0 per
cent (n = 316) work for the private sector. The public sector, more precisely,
central government, is second highest with 18.7 per cent. About half of these are
involved in the process of policy making (De Haan & De Weert 1990).[10]   A
secondary analysis of a survey among   graduates of the joint programme of
Leiden University and the Erasmus University of Rotterdam reveals that about 25
per cent of former students (n = 479) are working for central government, the
large majority in policy roles. About 65 per cent of the students working for
central government are involved in the process of policy making. Service industry
accounted for 17.1 per cent and local government for 14.6 per cent (Berveling &
Klaassen, 1996).

It is important to emphasise that the study of Public Administration is
relatively new. Graduates have to compete for jobs with their counterparts from
other disciplinary backgrounds, although relevant job announcements today
usually ask for graduates with a background in the study of Public Administration. As a result graduates in Public Administration now enjoy something of a
competitive edge over those who have studied more traditional disciplines.   For
example, the Department of Finance, which for a long time hired only economists,

now houses many people trained in the social sciences including the study of Public Administration. However, the number of civil servants with background in Public Administration is still relatively small.

The market for training is further supplemented by vocational training institutes such as the school for Hoger Economisch en Administratief Onderwijs (HEAO) in s' Hertogenbosch and the Thorbecke Academy in Leeuwarden which provide professional training in Public Administration.[11] The professional training centres have a wide appeal among high school graduates since the qualifications are not so high as for the universities.[12] A vocational training is often seen as a stepping stone for an academic education in Public Administration.

Post-Entry Training

That increasing attention is focused on pre-entry education does not diminish the importance of post-entry education. As we have seen in the section on MD programmes training and retraining is becoming more and more an integral part of 'being a civil servant'. Civil servants are sent to all kind of courses in order to maintain a high professional standard. In this sense there is no difference between persons recruited under a job or a career system.

Basically in a job system a civil servant is taking a course of training to adapt him or her to the requirements of the particular post. Looking at the 'short' term (function based) courses it is quite difficult to give a comprehensive overview. There is a wide range of training activities provided by all kind of institutes, ranging from computer courses, the development of management and personal skills, courses in personnel and financial management and introductions to general administrative law. Additionally in many departments new junior staff members will receive an introductory post-entry course on the nature and functions of the department and the style of policy making.

Training in the career system is not so much intended to improve direct performance but to prepare officials for their career in a particular branch of government. As said there are a few branches of government which still use a career system: the judiciary, the police and the military are the major examples. Although (especially in the case of the judiciary) a high level of pre-entry education is required the persons have to be equipped for their career by in service training. [13]

The police and the military training institutions sometimes recruit students with a completed secondary education. They are given a programme consisting of formal and practical instruction. Furthermore 'higher' police and military academies exist where selected individuals are trained for higher ranks. For magistrates there is an education and training programme (RAIO) where legal graduates are prepared for positions as judges and public prosecutors. In the Foreign Office future diplomats and officials receive a training of about six months after their selection.[14] The programme is provided by the department itself in cooperation with the international institute Clingendael located in The Hague. The institute also delivers short courses on international topics, for example to the Ministry of Defense. Finally, there are five co-operating academies of Public Administration geographically spread over the country which provide training for middle rank civil servants.

The differences between traditional career civil servants and the rest of the higher civil service are becoming smaller. The concept of management development is very much responsible for these changes. In addition some ministries - the Ministry of Education, Culture and Science, the Foreign Office, Home Affairs, Housing, Spatial Planning & Environmental Affairs - have started to appoint young university graduates considered to have high potential as (management) trainees. These are appointed for a three year period, receive an extensive training programme, and serve in different parts of the organisation (Home Affairs, 1997).

Training programmes focussed on career development are becoming more and more important for the whole of the higher civil service. For instance, promising higher civil servants with extensive experience in government are enrolled onto the Masters programme in Public Administration of the Nederlandse School voor het Openbaar Bestuur (NSOB/Netherlands Institute of Government) in the Hague or the Master of Business Administration programme of the Erasmus University of Rotterdam in preparation for higher positions. The NSOB is an initiative of several universities in the western part of the country. Similar programmes are also offered by the ROI, the privatised training institute for central government. Furthermore, The Netherlands hosts the European Institute of Public Administration (EIPA) at Maastricht which offers courses in Public Administration for officials of Western and Eastern Europe.

Turning to training delivery, four different methods can be distinguished:

1. Formal instruction by providing courses. The word 'training' often

suggests a formal and structured method of transfer of knowledge and skills. Courses provided or commissioned by various government departments, the ABD and other public organisations are obvious examples of this kind of instruction. Nevertheless in the MD programmes less 'formalised' methods are also used;

2. Training in and on the job. Starting a new job often means slowly becoming more competent in meeting job requirements. This often happens by way of trial and error. In the departmental trainee programmes discussed earlier this method is institutionalised and accompanied by more formal training;

3. The detachment of higher personnel to public and private institutions at home and to international institutions such as the European Union and the OECD. The approach is a more and more widely used method nowadays as most training institutes include internships in their programmes;

4. The transfer of knowledge, information and experience by the commissioning of research and organising of seminars. It is evident from the past that the use of seminars, contact groups and the commissioning of research has been and still is an important instrument for transferring information on the policy implications to a wider circle of government officials.

With respect to the provision of courses a distinction has to be made between those which are organised and provided by government itself (in-house production) and those which are contracted-out to external institutes. Contracting-out can take the form of a government department purchasing a course from a university department or a specialised public or private training institute, or sending civil servants to courses which are generally provided on

Table 4   Training Costs per Person per Ministry
(Millions of Guilders)

Number	Ministry	Costs
II	High Colleges of State	1.357
III	PM's Office	1.086
V	Foreign Office	2.139
VI	Justice	2.071
VII	Home Affairs	2.155
VIII	Education, Culture & Sciences	2.325
IX	Tax office	2.180
	Finance (department)	1.783
X	Defence	N/A
XI	Housing, Planning & Environment Affairs	1.070
XII	Transport & Public Works	.227[1]
XIII	Economic Affairs	1.539
XIV	Agriculture & Fishery	1.396
XV	Social Affairs & Employment	*1.735
XVI	Health Care, Sports & Welfare	1.576
Average		1.685

1.   The figure for the Ministry of Transport & Public Works is referring to the central training expenditure. Most expenditure is decentralized to the various departmental units.

Source: Home Affairs, Mensen en Management in de Rijksdienst 1997.

the market. Besides these general courses there are also many specialised courses provided on demand. In this sense a flourishing market for (government) training courses has come into existence over the last decade.

Government departments act as customers on this market and a wide range of public and private organisation as suppliers. There are special liaison officers, and often units, in each department and their counterparts in the training institutions are so-called 'programme-managers'. In the interaction the actual training programmes are shaped. This training market serves as a coordinating mechanism where central direction is lacking. It offers the advantage that training policies are more tailor made to the needs of particular departments.

Looking at the size of the market in financial terms, in 1996 about 189 million guilders was involved. This amounts to 2.3 per cent of the annual salary bill. From Table 4 it can be seen that there is a large degree of variation in the amount of money spent on training per ministry.

Conclusion

In this chapter we have used the metaphor of the market, highlighting specific characteristics. We believe that this metaphor provides a useful context of meaning. The market for civil servants trained in Public Administration is highly customer-driven and, therefore, flexible. It reflects the basic characteristics of the decentralised unitary state with its emphasis on accommodation and checks and balances. The fragmentation urges suppliers to adjust training programmes to the continuously changing demands of the public sector.

The demand side of the market has suffered an ongoing reduction of personnel. In addition, the government has issued an anti-recruitment policy with the exception of specific categories like computer experts. It has generated an internal market for civil servants that provides an impetus to in-house and mid-career training programmes (which are frequently contracted-out to the universities). The initiatives in management development and, more recently, employability embody and stress the need for an 'éducation permanente'.

On the supply side of the pre-entry market as a supplement to the university system there are a growing number of vocational training institutes providing training programmes. As far as the post-entry market is concerned there are a wide range of highly fragmented for-profit and not-for-profit institutes competing for the training of higher civil servants. The link between demand and supply in that market is very close due to aggressive competition.

Finally, we would like to emphasise the role of individuals in the development of the study of Public Administration. We have already mentioned Van Poelje as the founding father of the discipline. The next generation successfully spread the wings of Public Administration through their entrepreneurial spirit, moving from one place to another, and the establishment of new programmes and structures.

Notes

1. The poldermodel fits in the typical Dutch tradition of accommodation politics as 'coined' by Arend Lijphart. The revival is remarkable. The same politics of accommodation accounts for the Dutch disease of the 1970s.
2. The term 'civil servant' is used here as a synonym for public official. It covers the public officials at the provincial and municipal level of government as well as the judiciary, the military and the police. Furthermore, the employees of all kinds of semi-public organisations are not seen as civil servants.
3. The local government suffered even more since central government passed the burden partly to the provinces and municipalities.
4. The Wiegel committee estimates that the real 'hard core', i.e. civil servants involved in policy making of the departments stands for about 16.6 per cent of the total number of employees at the national level, though other numbers are sometimes given.
5. See for an introduction into the Dutch educational system William Z. Shetter, *The Netherlands in Perspective: The Dutch Way of Organizing a Society and its Setting*, Nederlands Centrum Buitenlanders, Utrecht 1997, p. 68-75.
6. The Dutch academic system educates for the so-called doctorandus-degree (drs.) that may be seen as the equivalent of a masters-degree. No distinction is made between graduate and undergraduate students. The first year is completed with a propaedeutic examination that performs as a selection mechanism for the remaining three years of the curriculum. The programme is completed with an internship that is an integral part of the Masters thesis (NASPAA Self-Study Report 1998).
7. He would soon join forces as professor of Public Administration at the Erasmus University of Rotterdam. See Daalder's memoirs (Daalder 97, pp. 219-221).
8. We abstract from PA-chairs in Business and Law Schools.
9. The concentrations focus on systems engineering, policy analysis and management.
10. The response was 316 out of 518, that equals 61 per cent.
11. In sum 4 out of 39 vocational training institutes provide a programme in Public Administration (see Annex 5).
12. The vocational training programmes stand for about 15 per cent of the total number of students enrolled in one of the pre-entry training programmes in Public Administration.
13. The judiciary, the military and the police are no longer seen as civil servants since the mid 1990s.
14. The programme has been under discussion recently due to a reconfiguration of Dutch foreign policy. A more individual training will replace the so-called 'klasje', that prepares civil servants for a job as diplomat.

References

Algemene bestuursdienst, (1996), *Plan van aanpak*, The Hague.

Algemene bestuursdienst, (1996), *Vooronderzoek. Internationale vergelijking van senior civil services*, The Hague.

Algemene bestuursdienst, (1997), *Verslag van de werkzaamheden 1995/1996*, The Hague.

Bekke, A.J.G.M. (1990), *De betrouwbare bureaucratie: over veranderingen van bureaucratische organisaties en ontwikkelingen in het maatschappelijk bestel*, Leiden.

Bekke, A.J.G.M., Perry, J.L. and Toonen, Th.A.J. (1996), *Civil service systems in comparative perspective*, Indiana.

Berveling, J. and Klaassen, H.L. (1996), *10 jaar gemeenschappelijke opleiding Bestuurskunde Rotterdam-Leiden. Een oordeel van alumni*, Rotterdam/Leiden.

Bressers J.Th.A. et al (1997), *Zelfevaluatie opleiding Bestuurskunde*, Universiteit Twente, Enschede.

Coolsma, J.C. et al (1994), *Een indicatief minimumpakket*, rapport van de werkgroep Bestuurskundig Onderwijs, [s.n.], [s.l.].

Daalder, H. (1997), *Universitair Panopticum. Herinneringen van een gewoon hoogleraar*, Arbeiderspers, Amsterdam/Antwerpen.

De Bruin, J. and Harberden, P. (1997), *Zelfstudie opleiding Beleids- en Organisatiewetenschappen*, KUB, Tilburg.

De Haan, J. and de Weert, E. (1990), *Opleiding en arbeidssysteem. eemn onderzoek onder afgestudeerden van de faculteit Bestuurskunde van de Universiteit Twente*, CSHOB, Enschede.

Gevers, A. (ed.) (1998), *Uit de zevende. Vijftig jaar politiek en sociaal-culturele wetenschappen aan de Universiteit van Amsterdam*, Het Spinhuis, Amsterdam .

Haan, F. (1998) 'Waar de wijzen in staatsdienst vergrijzen', *De Volkskrant*, June 6, 1998.

Hakvoort, J.L.M. (1989), 'Integratie binnen de bestuurskunde', *Bestuurswetenschappen* vol. 43, 1, pp. 21-33.

Instituut voor Arbeidsvraagstukken, (1992), *Mobiliteit van rijksoverheidspersoneel*, een onderzoek in opdracht van het ministerie van Binnenlandse Zaken, Den Haag.

Kickert, W.J.M. and van Vught, F.A. (1995), 'The Study of Public Policy and Administration Sciences: Context and History' , in: W.J.M. Kickert and F.A. van Vught (eds.), *Public Policy and Administrative Sciences in The Netherlands*, Prentice Hall/Harvester Wheatsheaf, London

Korsten, A.F.A. et al (1997), *Zelfstudie Bestuurskunde*, Open Universiteit, Heerlen .

Korstsmit, J.C. and Velders, B. (1997), *Action Plan for the development of a Senior Public Service in The Netherlands*, The Hague.

Lehning, P.B. et al (1997), *Zelfstudie Bestuurskunde ten behoeve van Visitatie onderwijs 1997*, EUR/RUL, Rotterdam/Leiden.

Lijphart, A. (1975) *The Politics of Accomodation: Pluralism and Democracy in The Netherlands*, University of California Press, Berkeley.

Maas, G.C. (1991), *Mobiliteit in het ambtelijk labyrint: over loopbanen van rijks- en gemeente-*

ambtenaren, Leiden/Amsterdam.

Maas, G.C. and van Nispen, F.K.M (1998), 'The Search for a Leaner, Not a Meaner Government', in: J.L. Perry (ed) (1998), *Research in Public Administration*, JAI Press, Greenwich (CT).

Maes, R. et al (1998), *Onderwijsvisitatie Bestuurskunde*, VSNU, Utrecht.

Ministerie van Binnenlandse Zaken, *Kerngegevens bezoldiging overheidspersoneel*, Den Haag 1976-1997.

Ministerie van Binnenlandse Zaken. (1992), *Management development in de rijksdienst. Een inventariserend onderzoek uitgevoerd door RPD-Advies*, Den Haag.

Ministerie van Binnenlandse Zaken, *Overheid en arbeidsmarkt*, Den Haag 1988-1997.

Ministerie van Binnenlandse Zaken, *Mensen en Management in de Rijksdienst*, 1994-1997.

Ministerie van Binnenlandse Zaken (1996), *Benoeming beloning en ontslag van top functionarissen in de (semi-) publieke sector*, Den Haag.

Nelissen, N.J.M. et al (1997), et al., *Zelfstudie opleiding Bestuurs- en organisatiewetenschap*, KUN, Nijmegen.

Rosenthal, U. (1983), ' De mandarijnen van de rijksdienst: modieuze stellingen en harde feiten over de Nederlandse topambtenarij', *Bestuurswetenschappen*, 5, pp. 302-315.

Rosenthal, U. and van Schendelen, M.P.C.M. (1977), 'Ambtelijke top in Nederland', *Bestuurswetenschappen*, 6, pp. 383-401.

Rutgers, M.R. (1993), *Tussen fragmentatie en integratie, De bestuurskunde als kennisintegrerende wetenschap*, Eburon, Delft.

School of Social Sciences. (1998), *NASPAA Self-Study Report*, Rotterdam.

Snellen, I.Th.A. (1988) , 'De grondlegger van het Nederlandse bestuurskunde. Het werk van Gerrit A. van Poelje', in: A.F.A. Korsten, and Th.A.J. Toonen (eds), *Bestuurskunde. Hoofdfiguren en kernthema's*, Stenfert Kroese, Leiden/Antwerpen.

Toonen, Th.A.J. (1987), *Denken over binnenlands bestuur. Theorieën over de gedecentraliseerde eenheidsstaat bestuurskundig beschouwd*, [s.n.], [s.l.].

Van Braam, A. (1957), *Ambtenaren en bureaukratie in Nederland*, De Haan, Zeist.

Van Braam, A. (1982), ' Naar een Nederlandse civil service', in: *Bestuurswetenschappen*, pp. 261-265.

Van Braam, A. and Bemelmans-Videc, M.L. (1988), *Leerboek Bestuurskunde*, Coutinho, Muiderberg.

Van der Meer, F.M. and Raadschelders, J.C.N. (1988), 'Political administrative relations in The Netherlands in historical perspective', in: F.M. van der Meer and J.C.N Raadschelders (eds), *Administering the summit in The Netherlands 1795-1996*, Bruylant, Brussels.

Van der Meer, F.M., Dijkstra, G.S.A. & L.J. Roborgh, L.J. (1997), *The Dutch Civil Service System*, Leiden.

Van der Meer, F.M. and Raadschelders, J.C.N.(1997), 'The Dutch Senior Civil Service', paper presented in the Whitehall project, Oxford.

Van der Meer, F.M. & Roborgh, L.J. (1993), *Ambtenaren in Nederland*, Alphen a/d Rijn.

Van Nispen, F.K.M.and Noordhoek, P. (eds), (1986), *De grote operaties: de overheid onder het mes of het snijden in eigen vlees*, Kluwer, Deventer.

Van Nispen, F.K.M. (1997), 'Anorexia nervosa publica. Een evaluatie van de grote efficiency-operatie', *Bestuurswetenschappen*, vol. 51, 2, pp. 105-118.

Waldo, D. (1955), *The Study of Public Administration*, Random House, New York.

Wiegel, H. et al, (1993), *Naar kerndepartementen. Kiezen voor een hoogwaardige en flexibele rijksdienst*, Den Haag.

5 The Unfinished Revolution: Public Administration Education and Training in Poland

JOHN GREENWOOD AND BARBARA KUDRYCKA

Introduction

Poland was among the leading countries of Europe in embracing modern democracy, adopting as long ago as 1791 a constitution modeled on that of the USA. Subsequently Poland experienced long periods of foreign domination both through partition - notably by Russia and Prussia, and which effectively meant abolition of Poland as a territorial entity throughout the nineteenth century (Kolankiewicz and Lewis, 1938) and through occupation during both world wars. During the brief inter-war period Poland struggled to return to some level of national independence. Of specific interest to the current situation of public administration is the experience of the 40 years prior to the reforms of 1989.

In 1950, a Communist government established a centralist system. As a result a unified state structure was established, the local agencies of central government were dispensed with and some local government responsibilities such as schools were removed. Elections in the one-party system consisted of ballots listing Communist - affiliated party candidates only. Dissent could be expressed only by crossing off names.

Several unsuccessful rebellions occurred in Poland during the 40 years of Communist domination. The significance and success of Poland's most recent reach for democracy, however, were unique both in terms of impact and scope. The national economy was heavily in debt and on the brink of collapse. Economic disaster provided the window of opportunity for political mobilisation.

The emergence of Solidarity as a unified independent trade union movement which demanded a wide range of economic and political reforms occurred in 1980-1981. The imposition of martial law countered public dissatisfaction but this was lifted in 1989 when Solidarity again emerged as a political force. 'Round Table' talks between Solidarity, the Communist Party and other groups in 1989 resulted in the legalisation of Solidarity and set in train a series of wide-ranging political reforms including free elections to the *Sejm* (Parliament), which Solidarity and other opposition groups were free to contest, and the establishment of a 100 seat Senate (now elected on a provincial basis) with veto powers which can be overridden only by a two-thirds majority of the *Sejm*.

At national level Polish central administration now consists of three competing institutions: the President, the Council of Ministers, and the various ministries. The President is elected by popular vote for a five year term and is titular Head of State. The first post-Communist President, Lech Walêsa, elected in 1990, was often in conflict with other parts of the government, and created a substantial presidential apparatus including specialists in various policy fields. Some clarification of presidential powers, however, came in 1992 with the signing of the 'Small Constitution'. Under its provisions the President has the right to propose legislation, and be consulted over the appointment of foreign, defence and interior ministers. The Council of Ministers, headed by the Prime Minister, is elected by the *Sejm* and served by the Council of Ministers Office, a substantial body which successive Prime Ministers have been reluctant to reduce.

The main effect of this phenomenon of competing administrations (Presidency, Council of Ministers Office and departmental administrations) is to create within central government both an incoherence in policy making and suspicion of rival institutions. These conditions, reinforced by the fact that most recent governments have been coalitions, and that non-Communist politicians will inevitably be suspicious of civil servants inherited from the old regime, seem likely to remain until final agreement is reached about the form of the constitution. In particular the position of the civil service remains confused. Not only is the status of the presidential staff unclear (civil servants or not civil servants?) but so too is the legal position of departmental civil servants. Politicians, in the uncertain climate in which they find themselves, have continued to interfere in civil service recruitment and to pack 'their' parts of the administrative machine with those perceived as 'loyal'. Many parts of central administration thus exhibit a partisan character. In addition there are continuing allegations of corruption.

Although it is widely recognised that these conditions deter many qualified candidates from applying for civil service posts, and also frustrate the promotional prospects of those lower down the hierarchy, reform seems likely to be delayed. Since a politically neutral and professional civil service, by granting job security and promotion by merit, would potentially weaken the politicians relative to their officials, administrative reform seems deadlocked. A further disincentive to recruitment is the poor level of civil service pay relative not only to that of the private sector but also in Poland relative to that of Parliamentarians (who have not been slow to vote themselves generous salaries and other benefits). Qualified people are not attracted to work in a discredited civil service under unsatisfactory employment conditions, particularly when they find themselves remunerated poorly relative to the politicians whom they serve, and when there is often the alternative of better employment in the emerging private sector. This has proved to be one of the most difficult elements of administrative reform in Poland and in Eastern Europe generally (Verheijen,1984).

The post-Communist reforms have also had significant implications for local government. Some 2400 new Western-style local councils or *gmin*, each elected for four years, have been established with responsibility for such typical local government functions as health, education, social care, housing, refuse, sewage, water, electricity, gas, communal roads and bridges, libraries and local transport. State (central government) interference in local matters has been reduced and councils released from much of the former hierarchical dependency for direction and decisions. There are also agencies (*voivodships*) which administer services between local and central government.

Public Sector Training and Reform

Poland was the first former Communist country in Central or Eastern Europe to take measures to reform its public administration. Political and constitutional change created a clear need for training those personnel now occupying unfamiliar or new roles within the governmental system. At the national level this was marked mainly by the establishment in 1990 of The National School of Public Administration. Modeled on the French ENA this offers two year postgraduate programmes for between 30 and 50 entrants per year. Graduates from the programmes are guaranteed a position in the civil service and indeed are obliged to serve the state for a number of years. While carefully modeled on similar Western institutions the annual output of graduates, around 30 per annum, is unlikely to provide the 'critical mass' necessary to quickly transform civil service quality and attitudes.

A professional training school for higher level officials exists, although, this became the victim of the stalemate in the Polish parliament following the October 1991 elections (at which 29 parties were elected). Attempts, particularly by universities, to develop in-service training courses for civil servants have largely been frustrated, mainly because uncertainty about the role and status of civil servants itself has become a barrier to designing appropriate training. In the immediate future, therefore, the development of in-service training looks destined for the same fate as civil service reform.

At the local level a more systematic and thoroughgoing approach to training has developed. While some training has been provided by *gmin* themselves, usually in association with other *gmin* or *voivods*, the main vehicle of local government training has been the Foundation in Support of Local Democracy (FSLD) founded in 1989 (Greenwood and Wilson, 1995). Non-political in approach (the first post-Communist Minister of Local Government - previously a widely respected university professor - was installed as its first President), the Foundation operates through a headquarters in Warsaw and some 14 Regional centres. Although its activities include information, advice and consultancy its main role is training; the target groups including civil servants concerned with local government, employees of the *voivods*, local government officials and councillors. It has also developed two-year training programmes for future employees of local government. Trainers are drawn from a wide range of sources: universities, overseas experts and local government practitioners (Greenwood and Lambie, 1995).

Training for the latter two groups, local government officials and councillors, was seen as particularly important. Under the legacy inherited from the Communist period, as a Western aid report described it, Polish local government 'staff accustomed to the superseded command system [were] ill-equipped and reluctant to tender advice, while [elected] members [felt] inadequately informed to make sound decisions (Amos and Gibson, 1991).

The role of local government officials in the Communist period had largely been restricted to implementing directions from the central government, an approach which discouraged initiative, goal-setting, responsiveness to local opinion and so on, yet many of these officials remained in post following the collapse of Communism. With elected members, 50,000 of whom were elected at the first 'free' local government elections in 1990, there was similarly little experience of Western-style democratic practice. Thus both officials and councillors were ill equipped to operate in the new democratic environment.

Training programmes offered under the auspices of the FSLD were, in the organisation's own analysis, primarily focused on facilitating the transition from a centralised socialist system to a market economy with regional and local diversity (Mularczyk). While there was heavy emphasis on technical skills - planning, accounting, auditing etc issues relevant to post-Communist reconstruction, such as public-private partnerships, encouraging local business, competitive tendering have also been covered. An early problem, subsequently recognised by the first President of FSLD, was that 'no education about local democracy followed' the initial local government reforms (Regulski,1992a), although this omission was subsequently addressed by drawing on overseas experience and expertise under foreign aid programmes (Greenwood and Lambie,1991).

While at the national level, as previously observed, political obstacles to civil service reform have impeded the development of effective civil service training programmes, at the local level, by contrast, where the creation of new local councils representative of local communities was a key element of Solidarity proposals at the 1989 Round Table Conference (Regulski, 1992b), training developments have been much more deeply embedded. While old attitudes and practices inevitably remain, Swiariewicz (1992) noted the emergence of two particular types of problem: one where councillors were unable to break the bureaucratic stranglehold of the old *nomenklatura*; the other where they tried to control every decision. Nevertheless there has been unmistakably more headway with training than at the national level.

Universities and Business Schools

In the Communist period education was regarded as an instrument for the development of socialist society. Industrial and technological progress was presented as a symbol of socialist advance, and research in natural sciences was strongly encouraged (Plaza and Kot, 1992). For the social sciences, however, there was much less scope for development. Criticism, open discussion and questioning the findings of empirical research could not develop within the confines of a ruling ideology. Elaborating official doctrine became the dominating characteristic of officially recognized social and human sciences (arts, history, linguistics, economics, sociology etc.). Questions of political and ideological purity became more important than issues such as scientific rigour, originality or quality of thought. Consequently, teaching and research within the social sciences increasingly lost touch with social reality. As an applied and practical social science discipline, Public Administration was severely affected by these problems and its development as a field of study within Polish universities occurred in virtual isolation from any contact with the West.

Even in the changed circumstances of the 1990s considerable continuity with the past is to be found. Many academics have remained in place, there is much continuity in patterns of thinking, and many underlying notions have remained. In many respects everyday academic life continues much as before, limiting the scope for change. There also remains much sensitivity to the moods and changes of politics, and anxiety about the risks of academic enterprise. The substance of teaching and research, therefore, may have changed, but its style, habits and forms have not - or, not yet. Old habits die hard, and the discipline of Public Administration - as a subject of potentially great political sensitivity - cannot detach itself from this wider educational context.

Nevertheless, several important changes have taken place. While economic problems have led to deteriorating working conditions in many universities, new faculty appointments, changed allocations of resources, and new 'power' relationships within many institutions have also brought change (and uncertainty) to academic life. On a more positive note there is now a strong desire to establish academic contacts with the West, and to participate in the international academic community, as well as a growing realisation that new political and administrative structures, developing public-private partnerships, and new management approaches have created a climate in which the disciplinary field is increasingly seen as relevant to the transformation occurring within the country. There is also some evidence that Polish undergraduates have adapted well to the reforms being well motivated by incentives in the form of monetary rewards, personal status and opportunities for travel, and showing not dissimilar characteristics to Western Public Administration students in terms of approaches to decision-taking, team working, diligence and conscientiousness. Indeed authors of one comparative survey concluded that Polish students were 'rated alongside the most decisive, the greatest risk-takers and best communicators' (Denscombe, Greenwood, Hart and Robins,1993).

In the past Public Administration was essentially studied within universities as a branch of law. It was taught mainly on graduate programmes usually within university Schools of Law and Public Administration: examples being found in Warsaw University, Jagiellonian University in Krakow, Lublin University, Wroclaw University, Poznañ University, Silesien, Toruñ, Szczecin and Gdañsk Universities. This is still largely true of University Schools, many of whose courses are still, at best, poorly related to the vocational requirements of the administrative system. Nevertheless, the quality of the programmes and staff is improving steadily, a number of new higher education programmes in Public Administration have started, and some university schools have recently changed their status to become Schools of Public Policy.

Alongside universities a number of private business schools offering graduate programmes in public management have appeared in the past few years, while the FSLD has been instrumental in establishing seven Local Government Schools all of which now offer undergraduate programmes. Although there is no obligation for successful graduates from these various institutions to work in the local government or civil service, most who finish their programmes do in fact enter employment within public administration. With the exception of the Polish National School of Administration, however, higher education programmes in Poland are seldom based on a comprehensive analysis of the personnel needs of state administration. Many argue that there is also insufficient emphasis on internships - vital if students are to adapt to the requirements of practical public administration without abandoning the knowledge and skills obtained through study and upon in-service provision for serving civil servants which is necessary to change the attitudes of those already employed. Even so it is encouraging that new training and education programmes in Public Administration are appearing, and are now being delivered through several different types of institution.

A major problem in the universities, of course, is relating teaching programmes to the needs of public administration. At the present time there is a demand for many kinds of skills, as well as for approaches, methods and techniques that are in their infancy in Eastern Europe (for example, business administration and management, sociology of organisations, organisational engineering, policy analysis, design and evaluation) and much of the existing literature of which is in English, French or German. In addition new systems and concepts of law have had to be incorporated into teaching. There is the further challenge for universities arising from the need to develop an identity autonomous from government and party, an issue of central importance in the redefinition of Public Administration, as well as a new, pluralist academic culture. Adapting to these challenges will take time. Much is to be gained from developing contacts between Public Administration teachers (and students) in Poland and in the West, but being in too much of a hurry could well reduce their effectiveness.

Because of these problems in Poland much remains to be done to tailor the programmes of Public Administration schools to the needs of public agencies. Only by defining the training needs of the public sector, and building a capacity to deliver what is relevant, are university schools likely to emerge as major centres for producing graduate recruits into the civil service and other public agencies. If they succeed in this the chances of graduates obtaining positions in public administration are likely to be good. Their task, of course, is exacerbated because the lack of political will to clarify civil service roles itself increases the difficulty of defining training needs, and also because there is no systematic process for communication between universities and other institutions involved in meeting public sector training needs.

Conclusion

Public sector training represents a crucial element in the process of political transition, for once the institutional system has stabilised, and the role of Public Administration been defined, the appropriate staff have to be recruited and trained. Unfortunately, in Poland, these preliminary stages have not yet been concluded. The absence of a final agreed constitutional settlement, and the low priority attached by politicians to civil service reform, has left public sector training needs ill-defined and the emergence of coherent and systematic public administration education and training consequently underdeveloped.

At some points, as this chapter has showed, progress has been greater than at others. At the time of writing the development of new education programmes in Public Administration, and initial and pre-entry training (especially for local government) has advanced reasonably well, but civil service training (especially in-service training) remains inadequate. The lack of in-service training is the more serious because it limits the positive effect of the influx of graduates from the universities and business schools upon the quality of administration. Old and bad habits die-hard and, if not countered by in-service training, can dampen the enthusiasm and impact of properly trained new recruits. The most urgent need here is to convince politicians of the need for administrative reform and to fund in-service programmes. Interestingly, a further obstacle is that high level civil servants and politicians are often reluctant to send staff on training courses, claiming that it will disrupt the work of the ministry. There is a role here for donor organisations to perhaps make their financial support conditional upon the adoption of civil service reforms and the development of in-service training.

While it is difficult to evaluate conclusively the various developments discussed in this chapter it seems clear from the Polish case that the effectiveness of public sector education and training cannot be divorced from wider political and cultural considerations. The huge changes in academic life, for example, have clearly impacted upon the discipline of Public Administration no less than in other fields, and have severely challenged the capacity of the universities to develop new Public Administration education programmes. With training more progress has probably been registered at the local than at the national levels. The political paralysis at the centre occasioned by competing administrative entities has, by stifling civil service reform and a redefinition of civil service employment conditions, made training needs much more difficult to identify and frustrated the development of, particularly, in-service training.

At the local government level, by contrast, much more progress has been made. A crucial factor here was the establishment of the FSLD as a non-political training agency, with substantial consensus about its role. No less important was access to considerable overseas aid funding, notably from the USA. Perhaps there are lessons here which are to be learnt if public sector training is to be effective in conditions of political transition and constitutional change. Where administrative reform is deadlocked, training is unlikely to be successful; where there is a political will to change it is much more likely to flourish. The central/ local divide in Poland offers a fascinating example of both scenarios.

References

Amos, F. and Gibson, J. (1991), *A Review of Support for Polish Local Government and Proposals for Assistance,* School of Public Policy (Birmingham University) (report prepared for United Kingdom Foreign and Commonwealth Office).

Denscombe, M., Greenwood, J., Hart, M. and Robins, L.(1993), 'Local Leadership Potential in Britain and Poland Compared: A Note', *Teaching Public Administration,* vol. 13 pp. 40-45.

Greenwood, J. and Lambie, G. (1995), *'Building Local Democracy in Poland: Training Perspectives from Western Europe',* Leicester Business School Occasional Paper 17, De Montfort University, Leicester.

Greenwood, J. and Wilson, D.(1995), 'Councillor Effectiveness: What Role for Training?', *Local Government Studies,* vol.21, pp. 432-447.

Kolankiewicz, G. and Lewis, P. (1988), *Poland: Politics, Economics, and Society,* Pinter, London.

Mularczyk, C. (undated), *Local Government Training Needs and the Foundation in Support of Local Democracy,* Foundation in Support of Local Democracy, Warsaw.

Plaza, K., and Kot, J. (1992), 'The Economic and Political System in Poland', in J.Regulski (ed.), *Decentralisation and Local Government: A Danish-Polish Comparative Study in Political Systems,* Roskidle University Press, Roskidle, Denmark

Regulski, J. (1992a), 'Grassroots Democracy', *Warsaw Voice',* April 12 1992.

Regulski, J.(1992b) *Rebuilding the Local Government in Poland,* Paper presented to conference in Krakow.

Swianiewicz, P. (1992), 'The Polish Experience of Local Democracy: Is Progress Being Made?', *Policy and Politics,* vol. 20, pp. 87-98.

Verheijen, T. (1994), 'Breaking the Deadlock on Administrative Reform in Eastern Europe', University of Limerick,1994.

6 Dealing with Rapid Development: Public Administration Education and Training in the Kingdom of Saudi Arabia

AHMED H. AL-HAMOUD

Introduction

Before the beginning of this century, the Arabian Peninsula was mostly characterised by fragmentation among various political entities throughout the area. The first Saudi state (1745-1818) was established by a coalition between Imam Mohammed Bin Saud, a political leader, and Mohammmed Bi Abdul Wahab, a religious leader. Both leaders were from the Najed region (central Arabia). The first Saudi state was ended by the intervention of the Otttoman Empire in 1818. The Second Saudi State (1840-1891) was established first by Imam Turki Bin Abdullah in 1824 by expelling the Egyptian forces belonging to the Ottomans; and then by the return of Imam Fiasal Bin Turki from his exile in Egypt in 1839 in which he regained most of the territory of the first Saudi State. In 1891 the Second Saudi State was taken over by Al-Rashied forces and imam Abdulrahahman Bin Faisal Turk went into exile with his son late king Abdulazize in Kuwait. The exile marked the end of the Second Saudi State. The Third Saudi state was established by King Abdulaziz Bin Abulrahman (known in the West as Ibin Saud) after his return from exile in Kuwait where he was able to take over Riyadh, the current capital of Saudi Arabia, in 1902; and subsequently he was able to unify most of the regions of the Arabian Peninsula under his rule. On September 23, 1932, King Abdulaziz declared these unified regions 'the Kingdom of Saudi Arabia', marking the official birth of the Third Saudi State. In its present form, the Kingdom of Saudi Arabia, occupies the main land of the Arabian Peninsula which comprises almost eighty per cent of the peninsula, covering an area of 86500 square miles (2,240,000 square km).

Since its unification in 1932, Saudi Arabia has experienced a tremendous transformation in almost every aspect of its life. However, even though this transformation was slow during the first four decades of its establishment, its speed has accelerated noticeably since 1970 with the launching of the first five year development plan. The sixth five year development plan was launched in 1994. The government spent tremendous amounts of money on the establishment of thousands of development projects. This has led to the proliferation of the government bureaucracy which is responsible for the formulation and implementation of those plans. Now the government machinery consists of various organisational structures which include ministries, general presidencies, public enterprises, agencies, bureaux, commissions, and province emirates and municipalities. Thus the number of civil service jobs increased from approximately one hundred thousand jobs in 1971-1972 to almost five hundred thousand jobs in 1993-94. Accordingly the number of civil service employees increased from almost sixty thousand employees to three hundred and sixty eight thousand employees respectively. The employment of non-Saudis has also increased noticeably during the same period.

The Discipline of Public Administration

There are seven universities in Saudi Arabia. These universities are King Saud University (KSU) in Riyadh, King Abduaziz (KAU) in Jeddah, King Fahad University for Petroleum and Minerals (KFUPM) in Dharan, King Fiasal University (KFU) in Dammam, Imam Mohammed Bin Saud Islamic University (IMBSIU) in Riyadh, Umm Al-Quara University (UAU) in Makkah, and the Islamic University (IU) in Madienah. Out of these seven universities, there are three which offer teaching in Public Administration. These universities are KSU, KAU, and IMBSIU.

The oldest of these is KSU, founded in 1955 in Riyadh (central Saudi Arabia) carrying the name of the second King of Saudi Arabia. The College of Commerce, one of its oldest colleges, was founded in 1957, two years after the foundation of the university. The College started to offer two undergraduate majors; one in business administration and accounting, and the other in economics and political science. In 1971, the college witnessed an academic reorganisation. Thus, the college started to offer four undergraduate majors in accounting, management, economics, and political science. The management curriculum was a diet of courses from business and Public Administration. The curriculum is designed so that the first two year entailed a common programme for all students. In the third year the student chooses to enrol in one of the two departments of the college, the Department of Political and International Studies or the Department of General Studies. The Department of General Studies offers three majors, economics, management and accounting. Students are expected to finish 127 assigned hours. In 1978, the College was renamed the College of Administrative Sciences consisting of seven departments. These departments are, Economics, Business Administration, Public Administration, Accounting. Political Sciences, Law and Quantitative methods. Since 1985, the College has required all students to pass compulsory courses in English language (14hrs) and quantitative methods (6hrs).

KAU was founded in 1972 by converting Jeddah private university into a state owned university. The College of Economic and Administration was founded in 1968 consisting of six departments; Business Administration, Public Administration, Political Science, Accounting, Economics, and the Department of Law.

IMBSIU is the third university that offers a programme in Public Administration. It was founded in 1974 through the unification of various Islamic Academic Institutions into one body. Even though the university was established to be specialised in Islamic education, it now offers a variety of programmes in the academic fields including Public Administration. It offers study of Public Administration through the College of Arabic Language and Social Science (CALSC) in its branch in Abha (Southern Region). CALSC was founded in 1976 consisting of nine departments. These are Arabic Literature, Arabic Grammar, History, Geography, Sociology, Psychology, Administrative Sciences, English Language and Translation, and the Department of Accounting. The Department of Administrative Science consists of two divisions; Business Administration (DBA), and Public Administration (DPA). DPA offers a Bachelor Degree in Public Administration on completion of eight semesters totalling 190 hours of study more than half of which are religion and language courses.

As is clear from the above, the foundation of the teaching of Public Administration as an independent discipline occurred in most cases in the first half of the seventies, and coinciding with the emergence of the early Five Year Development Plans. This is a reflection of the fact that with the beginning of the implementation of the development plans, the number of civil servants started to increase noticeably. Also, the qualifications and the roles required of those civil servants was becoming more complex than they once were. This factor, undoubtedly, was one among others that contributed to the foundation of the discipline of Public Administration. Therefore the philosophy underlying the discipline was shared in all three universities (see Al- Tawaih, 1995).

While the Division of Public administration at IMBSIU did not state any specific goals for the discipline, the two other departments provided some statements of their basic philosophy of the discipline. The Department of Public Administration in KAU, as one of the oldest Public Administration programmes, not only in Saudi Arabia, but in the whole Middle East, emphasised the goal of the discipline as follows:

- To present the Islamic contribution in the field of Public Administration.
- To provide students with the theory and academic constructs in the field of Public Administration.
- To present the concern of the Saudi environment during the presentation of these theories so to respond to the needs of Saudi society.
- To develop the students' skills and abilities in critical thinking and research methodology to enable them to apply them in order to solve administrative problems in the real world.
- To connect the Public Administration curriculum to the needs of the Kingdom's development plans in a manner which contributes to meeting the needs of local workforce.
- Heightening awareness of the concept of public interest and to construct civil service ethics, and to support the administrative reform process in the state.

Likewise, the main goal of the foundation of an independent discipline of Public Administration at KSU was to prepare a generation of graduates with the necessary knowledge and skills to support government agencies and corporations. Accordingly this goal can be achieved through the following.

- Providing an appropriate academic environment for the students to enhance their skills to meet the needs of the Kingdom's social and economic development plans.
- Preparing and developing academic programmes that can meet the needs of Saudi society.

- To conduct scientific research in the field of Public Administration on order to contribute to the process of development administration and to the development of the students' knowledge and preparing them to carry out their obligation toward their society.

It seems from the previous points that the discipline's orientation is concerned with meeting the demand of the development plans, but, in fact, we cannot say that its philosophical orientation is developmental since, in reality, there is no precise method to characterise its orientation. However, since most of the instructors of the discipline are PhD graduates in Public Administration from the West (Britain, and the United States in particular) most of the issues covered to meet this orientation are issues that have been introduced to them during their studies which have little relevance to the actual local issues that need to be raised in order to increase the students awareness of them. It could be possible, however, to say that the philosophy of the discipline is eclectic in nature, which is a reflected in the various approaches to teaching and which results in making them eclectic too.

Public Administration Education

As has been mentioned earlier, there are three universities in Saudi Arabia which offer teaching of Public Administration. Two of these universities, KAU and MSU, offer this teaching through independent departments located in Management Faculties, and the other, IMBSU, offers teaching through a division of the Management Department at the College of Arabic Language and Social Science. Both KAU and KSU offer Bachelor and Masters degrees in Public Administration, and IMBSIU offers only a Bachelors degree in Public Administration. The Department of Public Administration in KSU requires 48 hours of basic courses in administration, management, research methods, financial management and other related areas as a core course for the programme. It also requires the completion of 23 hours of basic courses in accounting, economics, law, quantitative methods, and computers as compulsory courses. In addition, completion of 18 hours of selective courses, half of them chosen by the student from the various courses offered by the Department, and the other half selected from a list of courses approved by the department are required of students.

Meanwhile, the programme structure at the Department of Public Administration at KAU is similar to KSU's. There are 68 hours of university and college requirement (14 hours University requirements, and 58 hours College requirements). The core course of the programme involves 35 hours of study. The Department also requires the completion of 15 hours of courses offered by other departments. These courses are government accounting, public finance, international relations, administrative law and computers. In addition to this, it requires the student to complete 18 hours of selective course work, nine hours of these courses must be selected from the list of courses offered by the Department, an the other nine are selected by the students from the various courses offered by the university.

The programme of Public Administration at IMBSIU differs from those at KSU and KAU in terms of its structure. It is structured on the basis of four years in which each year consists of two semesters. The students are required to take 97 hours of predetermined coursework as laid down in general University and department requirements. The majority of these are religious and Arabic language courses. After the completion of these courses, the student enrols either in the Division of Business Administration for a Business major, or in the Division of Public Administration for a Public Administration major. The Division of Public Administration requires the completion of a further 92 hours of a mixture of religious, Arabic, and management courses.

Both KSU and KAU offer Masters Programmes in Public Administration. Article (3) of the programmes regulations at KSU states the objectives of the Programme as follows:

1 To provide the opportunity for those individuals with a bachelors degree to sharpen their specialisation through knowledge and research in Public Administration.
2 To meet the demands of the society for specialised qualifications in Public Administration and related fields.
3 To promote the activities of scientific research concerning the practice and the problems of current Public Administration, particularly in Saudi Arabia and the Gulf States, and in the Arab World generally, and to contribute to the Arabic libraries in this regard.

In comparison the objective of the Masters programme at KAU is states as follows:

1   To promote the activity of scientific research in Public Administration and its application in Saudi Arabia; and to provide the academic environment in which to study issues and problems of Public Administration in Saudi Arabia.
2   To prepare administrative qualified personnel to be recruited to top leadership positions in government agencies and its various branches so they can possess the required qualifications to promote the activities of these agencies.
3   To prepare qualified and specialised academic personnel to teach both the art and the science of Public Administration.
4   To give concern to Islamic thoughts in regard to the different fields of Public Administration through research and the graduation thesis
5   To enable students who desire to raise their academic level through gaining more administrative knowledge and practical applications, and through the promotion of their analytical skills in the field of Public Administration.

There are some differences between the Masters programmes offered at the two universities. In order for the student to be awarded a Masters degree, the Department of Public Administration at KSU requires the completion of 42 hours. This is divided into 30 hours of required courses, including six hours for the thesis, and twelve hours of selective courses in the field of Public Administration. Besides this, the student is required to pass the comprehensive examination of the programme. The department of Public Administration in KAU, on the other hand, requires the completion of 36 hours. These are divided into 18 hours, and nine hours of selective courses and nine hours for the thesis.

In order to determine what kind of teaching methods are utilised as well as to gather other relevant information for this chapter, a questionnaire was designed and sent to the Chairs of the Department of Public Administration and Management Schools at all seven universities. All were filled and returned, except for IMBSU. KSU indicated that they use lectures, exercises, and field studies. IMBSIU generally relies on the instructor lecture as the main teaching method. Meanwhile through reviewing the available literature on these programmes, none of the three universities that offer Public Administration teaching requires internship as part of their programmmes' requirements.

Public Administration and Management Training

Public administration Training in Saudi Arabia is undertaken by the Institute of Public Administration (IPA) which was founded in April 1961 to be a central training agency for all government agencies (national and local). In the early 1960s Saudi Arabia was still affected by the 1957 financial crisis which led to various reform initiatives. In search of recovery, the Saudi Arabian government invited advice from a number of international experts in the field including the International Monetary Fund, International Bank for Reconstruction and Development, The Ford Foundation and a Mission of Experts of the United Nations. The foundation of the IPA was a direct result of those missions, in the hope that it could provide training services to public employees thereby increasing the efficiency of those agencies. The assumptions underlying the establishment of the IPA, but especially the value of efficiency, which is only one administrative value among many others, became a central orienting theme and a dominant one in guiding the IPA's activities ever since.

The IPA performs three main functions: training, organisational, and conducting research in Public Administration and related fields. Besides this the IPA houses the Secretariat General of the Higher Committee for Administrative Reform. In addition to its main headquarters in Riyadh, it has three branches, the Western Branch in Jeddah, the Eastern Branch in Dammam, and the Women's Branch in Riyadh. It has approximately 500 faculty members and training experts.

The IPA provides two kinds of training, pre-service training and in-service training. The pre-service programmes are designed to recruit high school and university graduates to be trained for one to two year before they can be employed either by the public or the private sectors. The subjects in this area of training include Business Accounting, Hospital Administration, Financial Studies, Legal Procedures, Materials Management and Secretarial Studies. There are other pre-service training programmes designed only for the private sector, where university and high school graduates are trained for two and a half years (one year of intensive English) before they work in various corporations in the private sector. The Training is conducted in English and includes programmes on Sales Management, Sales Operation, Banking Management, Banking Operation, Insurance, Hotel Management, Travel and Tourism operations, and other related fields. In 1995, the IPA graduated a total of 1,007 trainees from 45 pre-service programmes.

There are nine different departments at the IPA that provide training programmes. The Department of Executive Development Programmes (DEDP) provides workshops (3-5 days) to top management officials in both the public and private sectors. There were fifteen different workshops with a total attendance of 378 trainees in 1995. These workshops include Time Management, problem Solving, Stress Management, Leadership and Creativity, Performance Appraisal, Administrative Communications Skills, Strategic Planning and many others. In addition to this, DEDP conducts various seminars, symposiums and conferences in the practical field of Public Administration and related fields.

The Department of Social Programmes (DSP) designs and provides training programmes in response to special organisational needs not covered by the range of programmes offered by other departments. Based upon the requests of a given government organisation, DSP, in co-operation with the relevant training sector conducts a needs assessment at the client organisation. Based upon the results of their assessments special programmes are designed and provided for them.

The other department provides a wide variety of training programmes for government employees, ranging from periods of two weeks to eight weeks. In 1995, these departments offered more than a hundred different training programmes, attended by 10,675 trainees, with a total of 35,296 training hours.

The selection of trainees involves a process that gives both the employing organisation and the IPA a say in the training decisions of the employee. Thus, at the beginning of every academic year, the IPA sends its programme list to all government organisations, showing the titles, contents, periods and dates of the training programmes. These lists are sent to the different departments of Administrative Development in various government agencies. The Department of Administrative Development in each agency notifies the different branches and departments of their organisation which in turn nominate their employees for training. Each employee completes an application form giving relevant information needed to evaluate the applicants. These applications are sent to the Department of Trainees' Affairs at the IPA. The Department of Trainees' Affairs receives all applications according to the deadlines specified earlier, and classifies these applications according to the training programme. These applications, after their classification, are sent to the concerned training department at the IPA which in turn transfers them to the specialised training units in their department. The coordinator of each unit forms reviewing committees. These committees review the applications, and based upon the training programmes requirement they make their decision whether to accept, reject, or transfer the applicants to a different programme that may better match their qualifications.

Overview

The evolution of Public Administration education and training in Saudi Arabia has been influenced by two major events. The 1957 Financial Crisis mentioned earlier, and the launching of the series of development plans in 1970. The first event created a need to make the government machinery more efficient, thus, various international organisations were called on to provide help in this regard. This led to the creation of the Institute of Public Administration in 1961 and the value of efficiency became, and still is today, the predominant value guiding the affairs of the Institute. In order to achieve this value, the training of public administrators became highly focused on providing trainees with the skills needed to be more efficient in their respective government agencies. The Institute became highly recognised as a national centre, and its employees became the target for recruitment by other agencies to their top management positions.

With the institutionalisation of the IPA through the assistance of the international, mostly American, agencies new values derived from, and related to the core value of efficiency were introduced to inform the debate and determine the control and scope of training activities in the IPA. Many of these values were brought by the experts appointed by the international agencies and reflected the dominant values of their home countries. Those values include efficiency, managerialism, concern for productivity, Taylorism and scientific management. Those values provided a foundation for the new administrative structures of Saudi Arabia; but whether they have continued to maintain their formative influence or whether they have been transformed and developed different metaphoric significance in their Saudi Arabian context is still unclear and needs further study and analysis.

During the 1970s, and with the launching of the First Development plan, the financial situation was quite different. After the exploitation of oil and mineral resources the country became wealthier. The First and Second Development plans created tremendous demands for a more skilled and qualified workforce. The Third Development Plan (1980-1985) exacerbated the problem by questioning the continued reliance on foreigners to fill the gap between the high demand for qualified personnel and the low response of local markets. The universities developed programmes intended to contribute to solving this problem. In particular education in Public and Business Administration was designed to prepare individuals with more skills and qualifications to meet the demand. The universities sent large numbers of individuals for postgraduate studies in Public Administration, abroad (mostly to the US and UK). Those people returned to teach Public Administration; but with a spectrum of administrative values that are more relevant to the countries where they once studied than to the country where they now taught. These values found their way into the fabric of Public Administration in Saudi Arabian Universities and this deprived the discipline of the potential or capacity to reflect and enhance indigenous values and concerns.

References

Al-Tawail, M.A. (ed) (1995), *Public Administration in the Kingdom of Saudi Arabia*, IPA, Riyadh.

7 The Case of Malta: Public Administration Education and Training in Small Island States

GODFREY PIROTTA, CHARLES POLIDANO AND
EDWARD WARRINGTON

Introduction

Academic interest in the study of small island states has gained in importance over the past three decades. Much of this interest has been greatly encouraged by the emergence, since the 1960s, of a large number of such societies as independent sovereign states in their own right. Initially, much of the focus of the research was chiefly concerned with the question of their economic viability as independent states and tended to be rather prescriptive in character.[1] This has not completely changed but the fact that many of these states have managed to enhance their standard of living far beyond what was expected of them at the time of their independence, has helped to shift attention to other aspects, mainly concerned with issues of governance but notably Public Administration.[2] The Commonwealth Secretariat, whose membership consists of many such small island states, the International Association of Schools and Institutes of Administration (IASIA) and more recently the Commonwealth Association for Public Administration and Management (CAPAM), have all contributed significantly towards this change in focus. Other academic studies, with an emphasis on the politics of small island states, have also become more widely available.[3]

This chapter takes Malta as its case study. The Maltese Islands constitute, in terms of population (396,000) and geographic size (316 sq. kms), one of the smallest sovereign states in the world. Yet, although very similar in their characteristics to many other small island states that have emerged from under British and French colonialism in the post-war period, Malta presents some interesting differences. For example, because of its magnificent natural harbours and its strategic location at the very heart of the Mediterranean, Malta, unlike many other small island states, has over the centuries enjoyed an importance which is quite disproportionate to its size. Furthermore, since independence from Britain in 1964, Malta has played a role in international affairs which has been the envy of many other small states and which most of them cannot hope to emulate.[4] One reason for this stems from the fact that Malta, despite its long history of foreign rule, has an experienced public service which can trace its roots to the Middle Ages. But for a brief period between 1813 and 1836, Maltese Public Administration was nearly always vested in the hands of local public officers (Pirotta, 1996). It is this, perhaps, which makes the Maltese public service unique and distinguishable from those of other small states and indeed from that of many other former larger colonies. Nonetheless, like most of these latter states, Malta has a largely dependent economy, its most important mainstay being tourism. Similarly, like many other small island states, Malta is poorly endowed with natural resources and as in their case this factor, more than others, has generally helped to shape or condition its economic and foreign policy options (Warrington, 1995).

Over the centuries strategic considerations and the needs of a relatively large population have combined to give the Maltese public service a central and determining, at times even crucial, role in the life of Maltese citizens. Indeed, given Malta's near total lack of natural resources, economic development in Malta has been by and large state sponsored and directed (Pirotta, 1997a). And, in the context of this developmental process, the contribution made by the public service of Malta has been quite significant. The Public Service Reform Commission (PSRC), appointed in 1988, observed in its Report, that:

> if our nation's citizens are well-fed, well-clothed, well-housed, if they enjoy the benefits of education, good health and the protection of the law, if they participate in the creation of the nation's wealth, they owe something to the ability, dedication and adaptability of the public service (PSRC, 1989).

Of equal importance is the fact that the Maltese public service has long been a major provider of employment to a substantial proportion of the working population. Even today, at a time when expansion in private sector employment is at its highest, nearly 35 per cent of all those gainfully occupied are employed with the public sector, while a further 20 per cent or so of those employed in the private sector rely for their livelihood, almost exclusively, on income earned from government contracts and the provision of municipal services to the 67 local councils created in 1993 (Pirotta, 1997a).

Yet, paradoxically, despite its central role the public service has, over the years, failed to command sufficient interest either from governments, the principal users of its services and administrative machinery, or from academics, or indeed, its clients. We shall see therefore that, in Malta, government commitment to public service education and training has been both inconsistent and, until recently, inadequately funded. We shall also see that, as a discipline, Public Administration has not as yet acquired a distinguished place within the curriculum of Malta's sole university. The reasons for this are numerous and have been adequately explored elsewhere (Pirotta, 1997b).

This chapter cannot answer all the questions raised by these apparent contradictions. What it can and will do, is to examine the attempts made since the early 1950s, and their outcomes, in the sphere of Public Administration education and training in Malta. It will do so in three stages. Firstly, it will outline briefly the basic institutional features of Maltese government. It will then examine the ebb and flow that has characterised Public Administration education and training in the period 1956-1990. Finally it will explore two main issues: the position and career progression of Public Administration graduates in the public service of Malta; and in-service training for public officers since 1990. The recruitment of Public Administration graduates to public bodies and corporations outside the public service will also be touched upon towards the end.

Government and Administration in Malta

Malta's system of government and administration resembles that commonly known as the Westminster/Whitehall model. Power, for all intents and purposes, is vested in the Prime Minister, even though Malta has a President as its Head of State. Elected to office (and removable) by a simple majority vote in the House of Representatives, the President holds office for a single term of five years. The House of Representatives consists of a single chamber of sixty-five members, elected by direct universal suffrage, at five-yearly intervals, from thirteen electoral divisions under a system of proportional representation. The number of Members of Parliament may, however, vary from time to time because of constitutional provisions which seek to ensure that the party obtaining a majority of first preference votes also holds the largest number of seats in the House. [5]

Since 1947 Maltese parliamentary politics have been dominated by two political parties, the Malta Labour Party and the Nationalist Party, which have alternated in office at intervals of approximately ten years. Competition for power between the two parties tends to be exceptionally strong; for long periods the parties were under the sway of strong leadership figures, while over the last two decades both parties have constructed sophisticated party machines.

The direction and control of government is vested in a Cabinet of ministers appointed and dismissable by the President acting on the advice of the Prime Minister. All members of the Cabinet are members of the House of Representatives and hold their portfolios as long as they retain their seats in the House. Ministerial portfolios are composite: their contents are modified to a large extent with every ministerial reshuffle; the inauguration of a new administration generally means that the portfolios of the outgoing administration are dismantled and re-assembled in entirely new groupings (Warrington, 1995). Ministers are bound by the doctrines of collective and individual ministerial responsibility, doctrines recognised by the Constitution of Malta. The Constitution also legitimates the existence of a loyal opposition giving the Leader of the Opposition a consultative role in the appointment of members of certain independent authorities sanctioned by the Constitution, such as the Broadcasting Authority and the Public Service Commission.

The Judiciary consists of tenured judges and magistrates, who may not be removed from office except on grounds of proved incompetence, misbehaviour or inability to perform the duties of their office. However, such removal can only take place following an address supported by no less than two-thirds of the members of the House of Representatives. As noted above, apart from the Judiciary a number of constitutional authorities with powers to scrutinise and/or exercise executive authority in sensitive areas of public policy also exist. Others not mentioned include the Director of Audit, the Electoral Commission, the Employment Commission, and the Attorney General, but the latter only in so far as criminal prosecutions are concerned. A number of other Commissions or authorities, but which are not provided for in the Constitution, and which also have a scrutinising role, such as the Permanent Commission Against Corruption, and the Ombudsman, also exist.

The Maltese public service is one of the oldest of its kind within the Commonwealth of Nations. In its modern history the administration may be said to have experienced four main waves of expansion. The first occurred in the period after 1565 when an Ottoman attempt to capture Malta was successfully repulsed. From this period onwards the responsibilities of the administration extended to include the running of a number of hospitals and other related charitable establishments, a University of Studies, a national pawnbrokerage, a theatre, a printing establishment, several churches and the procurement, distribution and sale of essential food items such as grain. As the great landlord of the islands - one-third of all urban and rural property belonging to it - the government also exercised considerable influence on housing and land rents (Pirotta, 1996).

A second expansion took place in the period 1885-1938 at a time when the islands were under British colonial rule. British strategic interests, Malta being an important British military and naval base, and grave population pressures were at the base of this second expansion. The role of the administration now extended to include public health and sanitation, emigration, public transport, provisions of electric power and a wider provision of education. This new and expanded role for the public service was consolidated in the years 1921-33 when Malta experienced its first brief period of self-government. After 1947, during a second phase of self-government, the establishment of the Welfare State gave rise to a third wave of expansion in public service activities. Now hospitals and schools came to form part of a wider scheme of social provision which included old age pensions, sickness and unemployment benefits, and preventative health policies, notably in the field of polio, tuberculosis, dental care and infant health care.

The fourth and final wave of public sector expansion took place in the period which spans from 1964, the year of Malta's independence, to 1987, eight years after the closure of the British military base in the island. It arose as a consequence of Maltese governments' efforts to change the island's economy from one almost entirely dependent on British/NATO military spending to one based on light manufacturing industries and services, such as tourism. These efforts gave rise to new public corporations in the sphere of communications, energy, transport and economic development. They also gave rise to a substantial government stake, either through direct public ownership or in partnership with private investors, in tourism, manufacturing and service industries.

Although historically government in Malta has always been a highly centralised activity, since 1987 a number of measures intended to redimension the role of the state, have been taken. These included a limited programme of privatisation and the creation of 67 elected local councils - nearly one for every locality - with responsibility for the provision of municipal services.

The Maltese public service is also constitutionally bound by the classic Westminster/Whitehall doctrines of political neutrality and anonymity. The service is staffed by career officials mainly recruited through open competition and appointed, disciplined or removable by the Prime Minister acting on the recommendations of an independent Public Service Commission. It is divided into approximately fifteen major occupational classes and comprises over sixty departments, the Departments of Health and Education being the largest with over 6,000 employees each. Overall the public service employs in excess of 30,000 employees with another 3,000 serving in the armed forces. Another 15,000 or so are employed by the so-called 'parastatal sector' which includes within its ambit such public utilities as energy provision and telecommunications. Departments of government are under the executive authority of heads of departments and, since 1992, under the supervision of permanent secretaries. In the past heads of departments worked direct to ministers (Warrington, 1995).

But despite the approximation that Malta's system of governance bears to the Westminster/Whitehall model, significant differences exist in the way Maltese politicians administer existing governing institutions. Thus, irrespective of the existence of a number of constitutional and non-constitutional bodies and commissions, the aim of which is to obstruct political patronage and discrimination in appointments, promotions and government procurement, both of these features remain strongly entrenched in the way the administration is carried out. Both political parties have, for example, 'systematically extended government patronage by multiplying boards and committees, as well as by placing parastatals outside the constitutional safeguards for an impartial, merit-based public service'(Warrington, 1995). They have also colluded in carving out permanent *ad hoc* 'representation in bodies which the Constitution conceived as being independent and above party interests' (Warrington, 1995), such as the Broadcasting, Employment and Electoral Commissions as well as the Commission for the Administration of Justice which has among its responsibilities a role in the selection and disciplining of members of the judiciary.

This state of affairs went against the recommendations of the Public Service Reform Commission (PSRC) which was appointed in 1988 and which reported in July 1989. This Commission had clearly outlined the debilitating effect that such policies had had on the Maltese public service. Having done so, it then went on to recommend three vital changes: first, the restoration of the institutional fabric of the public service; second, the building of its organisational capacity; and third, the safeguarding of employees' rights.

Progress towards these goals cannot be said to have been evenly spread. For example, citizens have seen few improvements in the delivery of economic, municipal and social services by the public service. Nor has accountability in the so-called parastatal sector been significantly improved. Furthermore, it does not appear that public service management has become more effective. But substantive progress has been recorded in the field of information technology and human resource development, the latter having some relevance for this study. Indeed, one of the outcomes of the reform process was the establishment of the Staff Development Organisation, which has responsibility for staff training across the service (Warrington, 1995). A more detailed examination of the role being played by this department will be made at a later stage of this chapter.

Public Administration Education and Training: 1953-90

Until the early 1950s entrants to the civil service were expected to have an ordinary or advanced, depending on their class, proficiency in such subjects as English, mathematics, Maltese, typing and shorthand, and, but mainly at executive grade level, in physics, geography, history, book-keeping, and additional languages. Italian was included as a core subject in the 1960s while handwriting was also an examinable area. Candidates' proficiency in each of these study areas was tested under a system of open competition. A degree or another university qualification was accredited no weighting in civil service recruitment processes. Nor did Public Administration education enjoy any status on the curriculum of the university and very few graduates demonstrated enthusiasm for a career in the public service. Nonetheless, until the 1960s, employment in the public service was eagerly sought after by secondary school leavers because of the job security it provided, in stark contrast to other forms of employment, and the high esteem in which the service was generally held by the Maltese. Given this, in-house training was what new entrants could hope to get, although even in this sphere a short induction course was generally what constituted in-house training.

But the rapid implementation, after 1947, of an ambitious welfare programme and an equally ambitious economic development programme to sustain it, placed new demands on the Maltese public service. In the circumstances, governments became increasingly impressed by the need for a better educated and better trained civil service. This point was forcefully made by a Commission on the

Civil Service appointed by the Prime Minister of Malta in 1955. This Commission noted that 'efficiency at the highest level calls for officers of the highest quality and natural ability. The Maltese Civil Service is no exception. Indeed, we think that with the expansion which has taken place in recent years, there is the greater need for outstanding officers in the upper ranges' (Wilson et al, 1956). The Commission thought that one way of addressing this need would be by attracting university graduates to the service.

The introduction in 1955, by way of an experiment, of a competitive examination for the recruitment of graduates to the executive class proved, however, 'a dismal failure' (Wilson et al, 1956). In the first of two examinations held early in that year, none of the candidates passed; while in the second only three candidates sat the examination. The reasons for this failure, according to the Commission, were mainly twofold. First, that existing salary scales were not inducement enough to attract good university graduates to the service; and second, that the examination papers were not, as in Britain, 'aligned closely enough to the courses of study which the candidates had been pursuing at university'(Wilson et al, 1956). The Commission felt that a solution to these problems could be found in improved salaries for public servants and closer collaboration with the university in the setting of public examinations.

To date, neither of these issues has been satisfactorily resolved. While since the 1950s various reorganisation exercises and salary adjustments have been effected, graduates have, by and large, continued to look elsewhere for a career. Even in the sphere of examinations no significant collaboration has taken place between the university and the public service and the performance of university graduates in public examinations has continued to be below expectations.

Public Administration Education and the University

Given this state of affairs government ministers and senior officials came to the conclusion that a partial solution to the problem lay in a policy which encouraged serving members of the service to take up studies at the university. It was this policy which in 1956 gave life to the first of several fitful collaborative attempts between the University of Malta and the Civil Service. In that year the Department of Economics of the University, with support from the Faculty of Law, introduced a 3-year evening Diploma course in Public Administration aimed mainly at serving civil servants. It proved to be quite popular with an average annual intake, especially in its first years, of about 35 candidates. The general aim of the course was to help career civil servants gain a better understanding of economic principles, social administration and the social sciences. Hence subjects taught included economics, Public Administration, administrative law, social policy, sociology, history, political thought and Catholic social thought. The academic bias of the course was towards law and economics but, given that an unusually high proportion of the lecturers were clerics, Catholic social doctrine came to exercise a strong influence on the entire content of the curriculum.[6] This notwithstanding, the course succeeded in its aim of providing the government with better educated civil servants and it is significant that many of those who had followed the DPA course eventually proved to be some of its most competent and efficient leaders.

The success of the Diploma served to convince both politicians and public service leaders of the benefits of greater collaboration between them and the university and by 1969 a new scheme was in place. Under this scheme civil servants wishing to pursue studies deemed relevant to the needs of the service were, if accepted by the university, to be released from their departments on study leave with full pay for the duration of their course. The response of public servants was, once again, very encouraging and several of them, including a number of former DPA graduates went to university to further their studies, mainly in economics and the humanities.

This scheme was eventually discontinued early in the 1970s when a new Labour administration withdrew the sponsorships. A second form of sponsorships, which was already gaining in importance, was not stopped but severely curtailed. This was the practice of funding, through such agencies as the British Council, the Commonwealth Universities' Scholarship Programme and other international organisations, a number of overseas scholarships for serving members of the public service. Under this scheme a number of officers who had been successful in their degree or diploma studies eventually gained an opportunity to study in foreign universities, notably in Britain. Doctors, teachers and other professional members of the public service, had long enjoyed such opportunities before these were extended to general service grades.

Public Administration education once again found itself on the curriculum of the University of Malta in the late 1970s, although under somewhat unusual circumstances. In 1977, a dispute between the government and the Medical Association of Malta resulted, in among other things, the disruption of courses in the Faculty of Medicine at the university. The government's response to the medical profession's action was to create a second state-funded university and to introduce what became known as the student-worker scheme. The new scheme was eventually also extended to the elder of the two universities leading to their merger (Pirotta, 1997b). Under this scheme candidates for university places needed to find employers willing to sponsor them for the duration of the course before they could be admitted to university. As it turned out private industry was not prepared to participate in the scheme and the great bulk of would-be students were eventually sponsored by government departments, public corporations and other industries in which the government was the major stakeholder. For students the academic year was to be divided into two half-yearly periods, students being required to attend university for six months and to work for their sponsors for the other six. Furthermore, students were contractually bound to serve their sponsors for two years after their graduation. In return students were paid a monthly salary and had their employment guaranteed.

One outcome of these changes was the creation of a Public Administration Division in the Faculty of Management, itself a product of the new scheme, and the introduction of an undergraduate course in Public Administration. This course, as with nearly every other degree course under the new scheme, was of five year duration. It was to prove to be one of the most successful courses under the new regime and many Public Administration graduates were eventually to win scholarships which enabled them to pursue post-graduate studies in foreign universities. A large number of them also came to hold key public service posts in training, information technology, and offices concerned with public service reform.

The BA Honours Public Administration degree course, as it became formally known, was divided into parts. In Part One, which was divided into two semesters but which given the peculiar workings of the scheme was spread over two years, students were taught basic accounting, principles of economics, quantitative techniques and computing, sociology, elements of Maltese law, political thought and management accounting. With few exceptions these areas of study were taught to classes which also included students of accountancy and of management, in addition to students of Public Administration. Students who failed in Part One were barred from proceeding to Part Two of the course. Assessment in both parts of the course was by course work and by examination at the end of each semester.

In Part Two of the course, with one or two exceptions, study units were restricted to students of Public Administration. Subjects taught included econometrics, economic development, public finance, legal framework of Public

Administration, human resources management, industrial relations, social administration, government and administration, development administration, project evaluation, international business financial management, public policy and research methodology. Part Two was spread over three years with students attending university for six months each year, the duration of each study semester, and their allotted department or corporation for the other six. In each study semester students were expected to cover an average of four subjects and in the final year of their studies to write a dissertation on a topic of their choice. Students were encouraged to choose a research topic which had some direct relevance to the work place in which they had been placed during their work phase and to which most of them were to return after their graduation. But given the excessive secrecy prevalent in Malta and the reluctance of heads of departments to collaborate, very few students chose this option. And in cases where they did, the results were not encouraging.

The introduction of the worker-student scheme gave rise to heated public opposition. It was criticised because it restricted access to university education and because a rigid *numerus clausus* forced students to take up courses in areas of study in which they had only a secondary or even passing interest. The so-called work phase was said to be of little advantage to students, for except in a limited number of cases, few students were given tasks which had any relevance to their chosen field of study. In fact it was not uncommon for departments to engage students under their sponsorship on purely routine tasks or, indeed, menial tasks. Finally it was criticised because it tended to overburden the public service with graduates of all sorts, given the fact that the government was the overall sponsor of students.

Public Administration education was to be the first to suffer the effects of this latter development. Between 1983 and 1989, the year when the worker-student scheme was finally abandoned, the annual intake of graduates into the public service totaled about five hundred. But with the passing years the ability of the Maltese government to absorb the entire annual crop of university graduates into the administrative and professional classes of the civil service became increasingly strained. Furthermore, public servants who had served time in the service began to see their promotion prospects threatened by this massive intake of graduates. These fears were soon taken up by public service unions in their drive to ensure that at least half of those promoted to the higher classes came from among non-graduate public officers. In 1985, in response to these several pressures, the intake to the BA Honours Public Administration degree course was halted.

In 1987, following a change in government, the student-worker scheme was abolished. Students were to continue to receive a stipend but the concept of employer sponsorship was scrapped. The Public Administration Division was replaced by the Department of Public Policy. Courses run by this department came to form a Major within the Bachelor of Commerce degree, which had replaced the individual honours degrees in management, Public Administration, and accountancy previously offered by the Faculty of Management, now re-christened the Faculty of Economics, Management and Accountancy.

With the demise of the student-worker scheme students no longer had guaranteed employment with the public service and it would be fair to say that the vast majority of them did not see it either as financially attractive or as intellectually challenging. As the economy improved and challenging occupations became available, the annual trickle of graduates leaving the civil service turned into a flood. Attempts to stem the flow were made, especially with large scale improvements in salaries and work conditions, but the image of the civil service among graduates remained poor. Despite every effort made the exodus of graduates from the service could not be halted.

This state of affairs gave rise, in 1990, to yet another attempt at collaboration with the university. On this occasion, however, the preference of the public service was for the re-institution of the Diploma in Public Administration course rather than for a degree course. Initially, civil service leaders had proposed the setting up of an Institute for Public Sector Studies, but the university demonstrated little enthusiasm for the proposal. From a civil service point of view the re-introduction of the DPA course was a compromise solution.

The new DPA course was intended and designed for civil servants at mid-career level, that is for serving officers who were in the Administrative Assistant and Administrative Officer grades and whose ages ranged from 35 to 45 years. In 1994, however, eligibility for admittance to the course was extended to those in the grade of Executive Officer. The course was run by the Department of Public Policy and was of a two-year duration. Those admitted to the course were released by their respective departments for two working days every week. In year one of the course students attended classes in principles of administration, principles of politics, legal framework of administration, sociology, statistics, computing and economics. In year two subjects taught included contemporary administrative issues, decision-making, policy analysis, government and policy-making in micro-states, accountancy and a number of options from which students were obliged to choose two subjects. The bias in this course, as the range of subjects taught indicate, was towards politics and Public Administration, although the approach adopted was an inter-disciplinary one. As with other courses in the department, students were obliged to write a 10,000 word dissertation on a relevant topic of their choice.

The DPA course, as was the case with its predecessor of 1956-69, was initially very popular with civil servants and the number of candidates accepted was limited to thirty. The course was also rated highly by public service trainers and a number of practitioners collaborated with the Department of Public Policy as lecturers and tutorial assistants. But by 1994 interest in the course had declined. One reason for this was the failure by government to grant diploma holders either an annual financial bonus on the strength of their qualification, as was the case with degree holders, or to give this qualification adequate recognition during promotion exercises. Consequently by 1996 the number of diploma graduates had dwindled to thirteen. Since then no new intake of students has taken place.

In-House Training

In the period 1955-1990 a parallel could be drawn between the history of Public Administration education at the university and in-house training within the public service itself. During this period both suffered from a lack of consistency in their regard either from ministers or university authorities. It was the 1956 Commission on the Civil Service, the same Commission which had recommended greater collaboration with the university, which first stressed the need for a greatly expanded in-house training capacity for the public service (Wilson et al, 1956). The setting up, in 1957, of a Training and Education Division under Establishments in the Office of the Prime Minister demonstrated, as the launching of the Diploma in Public Administration course at the university had done in 1956, that at the time the political will to implement these recommendations existed. But the political turmoil which was unleashed in Malta in 1958 and the subsequent Emergency undermined these first developments and by 1967 very little progress had been registered.[7] Throughout that period the Training Division had only one full-time and one part-time officer engaged on staff training. The primary task of the former officer was to supervise induction training for recruits to the lower grades of the general service and for new appointees to the foreign service. In addition he was responsible for the coordination of a number of courses dealing with aspects of personnel administration, financial administration, and the conduct of public business.

It was not until 1968, four years after independence, that a more determined approach to training emerged. The catalyst for this new approach was Edward McCrensky, a United Nations regional adviser. The Maltese government had sought McCrensky's advice on the quality of existing in-service training arrangements and future needs. In a report presented in June 1968, McCrensky argued that Establishments Division, 'should devote more staff and other resources to identify training needs and to develop appropriate courses' to meet those needs which were service-wide. Establishments was also to work for the appointment of a qualified training officer in each department and to provide them with training, guidance and support.

He further recommended that all new entrants to the executive grades of the general service should undergo, on appointment, as interns in a variety of departments, a six months orientation programme involving both study in specialised courses and work placements. He also suggested that 'as part of the programme for training of public officials...planned interaction with officials of other countries' (McCrensky, 1968) should be established. McCrensky thought that this could be achieved through seminars involving interaction between senior government officials and overseas experts from selected countries; by planned visits to other countries for an examination of policies and methods relating to management issues and processes; exchange arrangements with public services in selected countries; and through government membership of such international societies as IASIA. McCrensky concluded, however, that such was the immediacy and the magnitude of the training requirements for the public service, that outside technical assistance was urgently required both in the identification of these training needs and in the drawing up of training programmes aimed at answering those needs. Following McCrensky's departure from Malta attempts were made to enhance existing training programmes. In 1970 the Training Branch of the Establishments Division held a full-time, month long intensive training course for officers in the Higher Executive grade. The content of the course was, by past standards, innovative and included sessions on modern management techniques, with practical demonstrations of the techniques in operation; visits to various industrial and commercial establishments, the purpose being to examine how these establishments were managed; and practical sessions which gave participants the opportunity to participate in group discussions and practical team exercises. The training division had also initiated a number of training courses for clerical grades and had, for the first time, organised an orientation course for candidates who had been successful in a special examination for university graduates. The novelty and the usefulness of these training exercises did not, however, mask the fact that, with one exception, Departments were not conducting formal training courses and that systematic on the job training was practically absent (Foster, 1970a).

Eventually, responsibility for the drawing up of a national training programme devolved on John Foster, another United Nations adviser. In his report to the Government of Malta, Foster distinguished between the training needs of administrative, professional and executive grade members, and those of departmental grades and clerical staff. He also differentiated between those types of training which should be the responsibility of the central training agency and those which were to be delivered at ministry or departmental level. He also proposed that the training programmes to be undertaken by the Training Branch of Establishments should consist of courses in management, financial administration, accounting, induction and personnel courses, registry training and, significantly, of training courses for would-be trainers (Foster, 1970b).

The public service was about to embark on the implementation of these recommendations when a change of government, in June 1971, as so often happens in Malta, put the whole programme on hold. It was to remain practically so until another change of government in 1987. From this period onwards, as we shall see below, but especially after the publication of the Report of the Public Service Reform Commission (PSRC) in 1990, the Maltese public service was to experience its first and best sustained training initiative in its entire history.

Public Administration Education and Training Since 1990

The remainder of this chapter is primarily devoted to two issues: the position and career progression of Public Administration graduates in the public service of Malta; and in service training for public service officers since 1990. The recruitment of Public Administration graduates to public bodies outside the public service is also touched upon at the end of this section.

Public Service Graduates in the Maltese Public Service.

In dealing with the first mentioned issue, it is necessary to outline the career structure of the public service. This is the fundamental determinant of the fortunes of public officers with degrees in Public Administration.

In the Maltese public service, staff have traditionally been placed in a number of broad categories according to their grade. The categories to which graduates may be assigned are:

- the general service grades (office support and middle management grades common to all departments);
- professional grades (lawyers, doctors, architects and engineers);
- departmental and technical grades (specialised career streams particular to one or a few departments).

The general service consists of around a tenth of the total strength of the public service. It is the group to which graduates in Public Administration are recruited, and is therefore the focus of this part of the chapter. At middle level management, its members perform a wide variety of general management functions throughout the public service. In addition, management specialisations such as personnel, accounting, finance and audit have traditionally been this group's preserve.

The general service stands out from the other occupational categories in that it is a single career stream rather than a loose grouping of separate streams. Being a single stream, it does not formally recognise its various management specialisms by, for example, placing accounts or personnel officers in a district branch. Moreover, a reorganisation of the general service in 1974 opened a single promotion path practically from the lower to the upper grades. Advancement was either by examination or seniority.

Paths to Top Management Levels

The career path from the general service to top management positions depends on the organisation. One may, however, generalise in relation to ministries on one hand and departments on the other. These two organisational forms are the primary building blocks of Malta's post-independence public service.

The general service has been the traditional recruiting ground for most top positions in the permanent structure of ministries. Indeed, the grades of Head I, II, and III (the latter being the highest level in most ministries, equivalent to permanent secretary level) were until recently considered an extension of the general service. Generalist dominance of ministries is, however, less than it seems: most ministries are transient umbrella structures within which departments - organisationally separate entities - carry the greater weight in both policy-making and implementation.[8] The only truly institutionalised ministries are the Office of the Prime Minister and the Ministry of Finance - central agencies with a service-wide brief over personnel and financial management respectively - and the Ministry of Foreign Affairs, effectively a department in its own right.

Generalists are less predominant in departmental headships, though they still occupy around half of all these positions. Generalists dominate those departments that have not traditionally been seen as requiring any specialist expertise. Senior positions in other departments, including some of the largest, tend to be filled from among the predominant specialist stream: for example, medical doctors in the department of Health, architects and civil engineers in Works, and teachers in Education. Headship positions in such departments were until recently classified outside the Head I, II and III hierarchy, effectively reinforcing the territorial demarcation at top management level between generalists and specialists.

Graduates in the General Service

Following the 1974 reorganisation of the general service, external entry at middle management level was opened to university graduates. Throughout the 1980s, graduate entry was linked specifically to holders of degrees in Public Administration, business management, and accountancy under the student-worker scheme.

Graduates in middle management encountered a degree of resentment from lower grade staff who saw graduate entry as cutting off their own promotion prospects. There are indications that the ill-feeling was also shared by some senior staff (Polidano, 1992). Such tensions are only to be expected during a period of flux and uncertainty brought about by changes to long-established patterns. The resentment towards graduates now appears to have abated due to both the passage of time, leading to greater acceptance of graduates, and the fact that - for reasons to be explained later - fewer graduates are being recruited to the general service.

By 1989, around 17 per cent of staff in the basic middle management grade of Principal[9] were graduates recruited through the student-worker scheme. None of these had yet made it to the level of assistant head - the level from which most department heads have been drawn - since promotions to this grade depended entirely on seniority until recently. This has meant that assistant headships and headships were, again until recently, the preserve of the rankers who were drafted into the grade of principal before the external recruitment of graduates began on a regular basis (Spiteri Gingell, 1990).

The net effect of this career structure, which has been described as it existed up to 1993, was to place strict limits on the importance or influence of Public Administration and management training at middle and senior levels in the Maltese public service. The first of the Public Administration graduates who were recruited in the 1970s and 80s are only now beginning to appear in headship positions, following the changes of 1993. These changes are described next.

Recent Changes

From 1988 to 1990, a wide-ranging review of the public service was undertaken by a specially-appointed Public Service Reform Commission. The Commission found deficiencies in management, going so far as to say that 'There seems to be little understanding of management concepts, and such management talent as has been retained is dissipated in "crisis management" arising from the predominance of short-term considerations' (PSRC, 1989).

It would be over-simplistic to pin a problem of such magnitude down to insufficient training in administration and management, and the Commission recognised this. Its recommendations did refer to training, but they also extended to career structures and promotions mechanisms. Considerable change has taken place within the public service in response to the Commission's recommendations. Two major reforms are examined here: the reclassification of top positions and the restructuring of the general service. A further element of the reform programme, the major expansion of training, is the theme of the penultimate section of this chapter (Commonwealth Secretariat, 1995; Polidano, 1996).

Reclassification of Top Positions

Over 1992 and 1993, a new top-level structure was set up consisting of three levels - director, director-general, and permanent secretary. These correspond directly to the old Head I, II and III grades, but incorporate most 'specialist' headships in addition to the generalist ones. A system of annual performance bonuses based on three-year renewable performance agreements was also made applicable to most positions in the new structure. New appointments are subject to renewal along with the agreement. It remains to be seen how the new structure will influence the career and educational backgrounds of future appointees to top positions.

Along with this change went a tightening of reporting relationships between permanent secretaries and their department heads. Permanent secretaries have a more clearly defined authority than the old Head IIIs, and the system of performance bonuses should strengthen their hands since their evaluation of heads' performance is a major influence on the award of bonuses to heads.

Restructuring of the General Service

At the same time as top positions were being reclassified, an overhaul of the classification structure at lower levels was also under way. An agreement with public service unions on the restructuring of the general service was reached in November 1993.

The agreement effectively split the general service into two classes, one comprising middle management grades and the other office support staff. A university degree is a mandatory requirement for entry to the middle management stream. However, staff in service at the time of the agreement continue to enjoy the right of entry to the middle management stream: entry to this stream is, in fact, guaranteed to serving officers who complete eight years' service at the top of the office support stream.

The middle management stream consists of two grades: that of Principal and the newly-created promotion grade of Senior Principal (the promotion mechanism being a written examination and interview). Officers in the latter grade are eligible for promotion to assistant director and, in addition, directly to the grade of director. This is a substantial improvement over the previous situation in which only assistant heads were promoted to directorships.

Contemporaneously, though for reasons unrelated to the reform programme, external recruitment to the grade of Principal was linked to a written examination in English and Maltese open to graduates in all disciplines. The opening of recruitment to all disciplines is a retrograde step for Public Administration, but it has to be seen in the light of prevailing circumstances: the termination of the University of Malta's Public Administration degree programme; its replacement by a public policy programme that produced only a handful of graduates each year; and an increasingly tight labour market, pushing private sector salaries into an upward spiral and making it difficult for the public service to attract and retain graduates in management or - even more so - accountancy.

The new general service structure gives explicit recognition to officers' qualifications and training. Qualification allowances are payable to officers who hold first degrees, masters degrees, or doctorates. These allowances are independent of career progression, except that the first degree allowance is not payable to officers in the middle management stream on the grounds that a first degree is already a basic requirement for entry to this level. Salary progression beyond the first four years at principal level is, in the case of new entrants to the grade, conditional on either possession of a postgraduate qualification or participation in an in-service management development programme. Only staff in the higher salary scale can compete for promotion to senior principal.

There are two problems with these arrangements. First, the concept that a first degree should not be recognised at middle management level as it is an entry requirement is dubious given that non-graduates make the majority of staff in the stream and retain the right of entry via the eight-year rule. Second, equating a post-graduate degree with a short in-service training course can give the impression that the public service ascribes low value to university education. This is unfortunate considering the paid and unpaid leave facilities, unparalleled in Malta, available to public servants following degree programmes in Malta and abroad; and the announcement in early 1996 that five MBA scholarships are to be awarded to public officers each year.

These problems illustrate the difficulty of binding training and education to career development in a situation where staff at the same level had widely different educational backgrounds and the interests of the less qualified are protected by a powerful union.

The net effect of the reforms are mixed in so far as graduates, particularly in Public Administration and related fields are concerned. The creation of the new top management structure is certainly to the advantage of the graduates who joined the service in the 1970s and 1960s; this group is well represented among the new cadre of senior principals and is poised to make significant inroads to the top management structure over the coming years.

In sum, the 1993 reforms have opened an accelerated route to senior positions for graduates already in the general service; but the recruitment of new graduates has been restricted and the balance of entry to middle management level has been shifted in favour of serving non-graduates. Unless the situation is rectified, a serious skills gap at middle management level will open up in the general service in coming years.

Expansion of In-Service Training

If changes to the general service structure have had mixed results, the same cannot be said of the expansion of training. Training has been one of the major success stories of Malta's post-1990 public service reform programme.

Prior to 1990, the Organisation and Training Branch at the Office of the Prime Minister was the central training agency of the public service. Given that this unit was around half a dozen strong, it was not well funded, and it was occupied with organisational reviews and other extraneous work in addition to training, it was hardly surprising if the organisation of training programmes was occasional rather than a constant activity. In 1989, 44 per cent of principals and assistant heads reported that they had not undergone any form of training in the previous ten years (Spiteri Gingell, 1990).

In 1990, following a recommendation of the Public Service Reform Commission, the Organisation and Training Branch was expanded, tasked solely with training, and given a more distinct organisational identity as the Staff Development Organisation. The new organisation was able to considerably expand the volume and breadth of training provided to public officers. In 1991, the SDO's first full year of operation, a total of 37 different programmes were organised for 2,313 participants. To put the latter figure in perspective, it is equivalent to 16 per cent of the total strength of the public service.

Training courses organised by the Staff Development Organisation cover a very wide field, going from word-processing to 'pure' academic subjects such as economics, although the emphasis is very much on 'practical' skills and procedural knowledge. Nevertheless, it is difficult to arrive at a hard-and-fast categorisation of courses in terms of knowledge or skills owing to the wide variety of courses and the difficulty of defining these terms with sufficient precision.

Instead, the following categorisation was felt to better reflect the diversity of training being provided:

- academic subjects such as economics, Public Administration, and law, or management disciplines that would be a central part of a university degree programme, such as personnel, financial, operations and project management, or aspects therefore;
- aspects of management that are more properly considered 'skills', though even they may well form part of a university degree programme, such leadership, supervision, change management, or time management;[10]
- other skills (language, report writing, making presentations, office support, and customer services);
- training related to major government policy initiatives (gender issues, TU familiarisation, VAT, and local council management);
- familiarisation with administrative systems specific to the Maltese public service (budgeting, business planning, financial and personnel administration procedures, the archiving of records, and various department-specific work procedures);
- training in the use of IT applications (word processing, spreadsheet, databases, and more specialised software).

These groupings are fairly loose and involve an element of arbitrariness as many courses do not clearly fit into any one category. Taken together, however, they give a fairly good overview of the extent of SDO training. Many of the courses are developed and delivered using the SDO's own resources, while others rely on inputs from other government organisations such as the Management Systems Unit or are commissioned from private training organisations. The chart below provides a percentage breakdown of participants according to the categories set out above, though the percentages should be taken as indications rather than precise figures owing to the difficulty of precise categorisation.

It is apparent that, going by the percentage of participants, the weight of SDO's training effort is concentrated in two main areas: IT training and familiarisation with administrative systems. The large effort put into IT training reflects the scale of the investment in information technology and systems development in government departments as well as long pent-up demand for such training. Before the post-1990 reform effort got under way, the use of information technology in government was very limited. The changes currently taking place in

Table 1   Participants in SDO training, by percentage according to category

Category of training.	1991	1992	1993	1994	1995	Avg.
Academic disciplines	9	4	2	1	8	5
Management Skills	15	14	9	5	5	8
Other skills	4	13	5	7	16	10
Policy related	5	1	14	17	3	9
Administrative systems	43	40	11	14	20	23
IT applications	24	28	59	56	48	45
Numerical total	**2313**	**3409**	**4049**	**5873**	**5341**	**20,985**

this area represent what is probably the outstanding success story of the post-1990 reform programme.

In the case of familiarisation with administrative systems, the bulk of participation actually represents induction or promotion courses for newly appointed staff. But around a third of the activity in this area represents training in support of the introduction of new systems, such as business planning or performance management, that are a direct outcome of reform initiatives. The SDO's activities are conditioned mainly by the public service effort, out of which the organisation itself was born.

Training for Senior and Middle Management

An important early focus for the Staff Development Organisation's activities was management development training for senior staff, though this does not show up in the figures owing to the relatively small numbers involved compared with, say, IT training. Again, this was in support of a key priority of the reform programme - the strengthening of departmental management. At the outset. the decision was taken not to distinguish between managers with a general serv ce or a specialist background: both groups were exposed to the same training. The training in question revolved around two programmes, Developing Leadership Skills and Managing Change. These programmes were later extended to lower levels and finally halted when the potential target population had been covered.

Currently, there is no specific programme of in-service management training which each officer in a senior or middle management grade can expect to undergo, though training opportunities continue to be offered to such levels on an ad hoc basis. Participation in courses is either voluntary (IT, and skills) or on the nomination of heads of department (many 'academic' and management skills programmes) or according to functional role (policy-related training and system familiarisation).

Training and Reform

The closer relationship between in-service training and public service reform in Malta raises the issue of whether or to what extent training can be considered as a catalyst of reform. A number of authors discount this idea, saying that training on its own is a weak lever for change.[11] Malta's experience confirms this general tenet, if confirmation is needed. To be effective, training must take place in a context of systematic change: the SDO's IT training, for example, succeeded because it took place in the context of investment in equipment, computerisation of major departmental systems, and the provision of technical support. Reform is all about providing that context, and providing it requires the investment of considerable funds, effort and political capital. In the absence of that investment, new skills will remain unused and may be forgotten in short order (Commonwealth Secretariat, 1995).

Another dubious notion is that of training as a catalyst - that change will take place on its own if a critical mass of trained staff is built up. In practice, this is a very doubtful proposition. The concept assumes that those trained will automatically accept the new ideas to which they are exposed: inconvenient attitudes or beliefs are not so easy to educate away. Even aside from this problem, the mere gathering of people with new ideas will rarely lead to change except over a very long time-frame - generations rather than years - and with the help of other contingent factors, such as the emergence of a leader who can unify those in favour of change, translate their ideas into a tangible set of proposals for change, and focus their energies on the realisation of those proposals.[12] Training alone is no painless shortcut to change.

Public Administration Education in the Wider Public Sector

The discussion so far has centred on the public service itself - the core of the public sector. This is with reason. Little importance has been attached to education in Public Administration outside that core, that is to say in statutory public corporations, non-statutory public bodies outside the public service, state-owned limited liability companies, and local councils.

When recruiting general management staff, the most common practice among these organisations appears to be that of asking for business management or related qualifications, or else not to specify what disciplines are sought. This is not to say that graduates in Public Administration or public policy are excluded from such organisations: many, especially of the first-named disciplines, are to be found throughout the public sector. It does mean, however, that prospective university students may opt for a commerce or business management programme in the belief that this will offer them more job opportunities even within the public sector.

The situation where local councils are concerned remains too fluid three years after their establishment for an assessment to be made. Council secretaries (chief administrators) were initially mainly seconded public officers from the general service, though few if any graduates were among those seconded. An extensive programme of training in council operations and management was organised for this group by the SDO. Since then, many councils have begun advertising publicly to fill secretaryships that fell vacant. The norm here appears to be not to indicate any preference as qualifications.   The tight labour market may be leaving the councils with no other option: one council had to advertise repeatedly to find any suitable candidates at all.[13]

The special problems of councils apart, there may be a chicken-and-egg situation with respect to the establishment of Public Administration as a viable discipline for those seeking a career in the public sector. In the absence of a well-established BA or Masters degree programme producing a sizable group of graduates each year, employers will not include the discipline in their graduate-level recruitment plans; but unless they do so, it will be difficult for a university programme in the field to attract enough students and establish itself on a secure footing.

Conclusion

In small states public services tend to play a vital and central role in the socio-economic life of their communities, a fact which is also true of Malta. But, as this account has demonstrated, in Malta there was neither a systematic nor a consistent approach to Public Administration education and training. The University of Malta, though willing to assist the public service in the development of its officers, proved most of the time to be a disinterested partner. This may also explain the attitude of graduates towards the public service. Graduates failed to conceive of the public service as a profession in its own right. Indeed, many of them saw it merely as an employment which appealed to secondary school leavers and sixth formers.

But, even in the case of in-house training, we have seen that despite a number of earlier attempts, until the 1990s and the creation of the Staff Development Organisation (SDO), very little had been achieved. The attitude of different governments to the importance, or lack of it, of training has not helped and it will be some time before the long term impact of present training strategies can be fully assessed, provided that present programmes are maintained and expanded.

Notes

1. See, for example, Lee, J.M. (1967), *Colonial Development and Good Government*, Clarendon Press, Oxford; Benedict, B. (ed.), (1967), *Problems of Smaller Territories*, Athlone Press, London; Commonwealth Secretariat, (1985), *Vulnerability: Small States in the Global Village*, Commonwealth Secretariat, London; and Kaminarides, J., Brigulio, L., and Hoogendonk, H. (eds), (1989), *The Economic Development of Small Countries: Problems, Strategies and Policies*, Nl:Euburon, Delft.
2. See Baker, R. (ed.), (1992), *Public Administration in Small and Island States*, Kumanarian Press, West Harford, U.S.A.; Dommen, E. and Hein, P. (eds), (1985), *States, Microstates and Islands*, Croom Helm, London; and Ghai, Y. (ed), (1990), *Public Administration and Management in Small States: Pacific Experiences*, Commonwealth Secretariat, London.
3. See, for example, Clarke, C. and Payne, A. (eds), (1987), *Politics, Security and Development of Small States*, Allen & Unwin, London; and Payne, A. and Sutton, P. (1993), *Modern Caribbean Politics*, Johns Hopkins University Press, Maryland, USA.
4. Since its independence Malta has been an active member of several international organisations such as the United Nations, the Council of Europe, and the Movement of Non-Aligned. Within each of these bodies it has been responsible for a number of world-wide initiatives such as the International Law of the Sea Convention, the Rights of Future Generations initiative and the Mediterranean Dimension clause in the Helsinki Treaty on

Security and Co-operation in Europe. Malta is also a central player in the Euro-Mediterranean process currently underway between the European Union and other non-member states.

5. Despite having a system of proportional representation, frequent changes to constituency boundaries have eroded this proportionality resulting in Constitutional provisions which aim to ensure that the party polling fifty-one percent of the votes casts gains at least a one seat majority in Parliament.

6. This observation is based on information obtained from public servants who had followed the DPA course.

7. In 1958 serious rioting occurred in Malta after the British Government declared its intention to privatise its naval dockyard Malta. The dockyard was at the time Malta's largest single employer. The riots led to the resignation of the island's elected government and the re-imposition of direct British rule.

8. This reflects the institutional history of Maltese government: many departments date back to the early British colonial era and their heads, main Maltese, played an instrumental role in colonial governance, whereas ministries are essentially creatures of independence. For a full account of the development and the role of the Maltese public service see Pirotta, G.A. (1996), *The Maltese Public Service 1800-1940: The Administrative Politics of a Micro-State*, Mireva Publications, Malta.

9. Strictly speaking, the grade of Principal was known as administrative officer prior to 1993. In this chapter grade titles have been standardised to avoid confusion.

10. University programmes may place emphasis on theory and research findings, whereas in-service courses - even though they may draw on the same materials - tend to focus more on 'how to' skills that can be applied in the workplace.

11. Among others, Wilenski, P. (1986), 'Administrative Reform - General Principles and the Australian Experience', *Public Administration*, vol. 64, 3; Holmes, M. (1982), 'Public Sector Management Reform: Convergence or Divergence?', *Governance*, vol. 5, 4; and Hofstede, G. (1991), *Cultures and Organisations: Software of the Mind*, McGraw-Hill, London.

12. In Britain, for instance, the ideas propagated by the Fulton Committee in its 1968 report only found fruition in the management reforms of a decade and a half later.

13. This was stated by Paul Fenech, the elected Mayor of Swieqi, in Malta, in a letter to the *Sunday Times* (Malta) of the 4th Febuary 1996.

References

Foster, J. W. (1970a), *First Periodic Report by the United Nations Civil Service Training Adviser*, Malta Government, Malta.

Foster, J. W. (1970b), *A National Programme for Training in Public Administration*, Malta Government, Malta.

McCrensky, E. (1968), *Report of the Special Adviser on Training in the Public Service of Malta to the Prime Minister*, Malta Government, Malta.

Pirotta, G. A. (1996), *The Maltese Public Service 1800-1940: The Administrative Politics of a Micro-State*, Mireva Publications, Malta.

Pirotta, G.A. (1997a), 'Politics and Public Service Reform in Small States: Malta', *Public Administration and Development*, vol. 17, 1, pp. 177-207.

Pirotta, G. A. (1997b), 'The Disciplines of Politics and Public Administration in Malta', *Teaching Public Administration,* vol. 17, 1, pp. 1-20.

Polidano, C. (1992), 'Caught in a Double Bind: The Cultural Pitfalls Facing Public Service Reformers', *Administrative Review,* no. 2, pp. 15-18.

Polidano, C. (1996), 'Public Service Reform in Malta, 1989-95: Lessons To Be Learned', *Governance,* vol. 9, 4, pp. 459-480.

Public Service Reform Commission, (1989), *A New Public Service for Malta: A Report on the Organisation of the Public Service,* Malta Government, Malta.

Spiteri Gingell, D. (1990), 'Survey of General Service Officers: A Preliminary Report', in *A New Public Service for Malta: Supplementary Papers,* Malta Government, Malta.

Warrington, E. (ed), (1995), 'Introduction' in *Current Good Practices and New Developments in Public Service Management: A Profile of the Public Service of Malta,* Commonwealth Secretariat, London.

Wilson, A., Day, A. and Whitehead, A. S. (1956), *Report of the Commission on the Malta Civil Service,* Department of Information, Malta.

8 Combining Democracy, Rule of Law and Efficiency: Public Administration Education and Training in Sweden

KERSTIN KOLAM

Introduction

Defining Public Administration programmes in Sweden is not an easy task. Apart from the programmes that are labelled Public Administration, there are also other university programmes that both consist of Public Administration courses and aim at employment within public administration. The programme for social work, for example, has courses in political science, law and economics where the students learn about the Swedish public system, legal aspects and public economy. The students are employed mainly by local authorities. Other examples are the environmental health programme and the programme for human resources management and development.

Some state authorities, like the police, the customs, the military, and the National Post and Telecom Agency have colleges of their own, for example the National Defence College. But in the main the state relies on the education that is provided by universities. In some cases a university degree is a requirement for access to these types of in-service training. It would, thus, take us too far to describe all such programmes. Therefore, this article only deals with 'pure' Public Administration programmes.

In Sweden, Public Administration is regarded as a sub-discipline of political science. Almost all programmes have a set of core subjects that are compulsory. The most common core subjects are political science and economics. Depending on the university the students may also choose statistics, sociology, business administration or social and economic geography as their major subject.

Since Public Administration is regarded as a sub-discipline of political science, it is also mainly in this subject that Public Administration perspectives are to be found. Some other subjects, such as law and statistics also contain elements on Public Administration but these subjects are not dealt with here.

Sweden's Politico-Administrative System

Sweden is a parliamentary democracy with a unicameral Parliament (*Riksdag*) as the supreme decision-making body (Petersson,1994; Statskontoret, 1998). The Parliament, consisting of 349 members, is elected every fourth year. It is the most gender-equal parliamentary assembly in the world with some 43 per cent of women MPs. The head of the State, King Carl XVI Gustaf, does not exercise any political power.

The Government Chancery includes the Cabinet Office, the Government Administrative Office and, at present, 11 Ministries. The number of employees is low in international terms, i.e. less than 2,000 people. The majority of national government (State) employees are to be found in the government administrative agencies, which are independent from the ministries. State tasks include foreign policy and defence, public order and security, the judicial system, macro economic policy, higher education and research, highways and long distance transportation and communication, labour market policy and employment issues, housing policy, social insurance and transfer payments (Häggroth et al, 1983).

At regional level there are some 20 County Administrative Boards, one in each county, directly subordinate to the Government and headed by a County Governor, who is appointed by the Government. The 14 members of the County Board are appointed by the County Council in the region . Some public authorities have local agencies, for example post offices, public employment agencies etc.

There are two types of local government in Sweden: 288 municipalities and 21 county councils. The latter operate at the regional level and have health care as their main responsibility, but they are also involved with the care of the mentally retarded, cultural activities, public transport etc. Municipalities are in charge of a broad range of tasks: social services, education, recreation and culture, technical services (streets, energy, water and sewage etc), environment and public health, civil defence, local communications, and planning. Some of the tasks are compulsory (about 80 per cent) and some optional. In conclusion, one might say that the major part of the public service that affects the everyday life of the citizen is carried out by the municipalities and county councils.

Both municipalities and county councils have elected assemblies as the highest decision-making body. Elections are held every fourth year, on the same day as parliamentary elections. The Executive Committee, appointed by the Council, is the highest governing body. In addition there are varying numbers of committees and boards. Every municipality and county council has full freedom to organise activities according to its own needs. The local governments do not, however, operate separately from one another. There is a close co-operation between municipalities, the County Council and the County Administrative Board in each region.

Local governments derive their revenue mainly from local income tax (about 50-55 per cent in the case of municipalities and 70-80 per cent with county councils) and from State bloc grants (some 20-25 per cent) (Häggroth et al, 1992). Every local unit has a constitutional right to determine the rate of income tax. This right is regarded as one of the cornerstones for Swedish local self-government and local democracy.

Some characteristics of Swedish public administration are worthy of emphasis. The Freedom of the Press Act includes the principle of public access. All documents kept at public agencies are available for citizens to peruse. Material classified as secret are the exceptions to this rule. Persons who wish to view public documents do not have to state their motives for this or identify themselves. The principle of public access is an important part of the 'open Swedish society'. This right is, naturally, mostly exercised by the media.

Legislation has changed character during the past decades from detailed regulations to framework laws. One obvious advantage is that laws do not have to be changed that frequently. The new type of generally formulated laws permit some variations at local level. Municipalities and county councils may adapt the rules according to their local contexts. But this approach also creates a higher responsibility for public servants, who may have to interpret laws in their daily activities.

Finally, it is important to mention that public administration is the largest employer of women. Sweden is claimed to have the most segregated labour market in the world. As in all Nordic countries women are to be found in care and men in manufacturing at the labour market, but more so in Sweden than in the other countries. The present situation is like a Catch-22 case:

women need the services provided for by the public sector in order to take part in working life; at the labour market they often work within these services. Recent cutbacks in public financing, thus, have a twofold effect on women. Some positive changes are also underway. The equal opportunities policy, which requires a written document in every workplace (including the private sector) with more than ten employees, is gradually affecting the distribution among men and women in higher administrative positions. According to the 1998 Human Development Report almost 40 per cent of persons in administrative and managerial positions are women (UNDP, 1998).

Public Administration in Sweden

Sweden has one of the largest public sectors in the world, both in terms of expenditure and numbers of employees. A large public sector was considered to be one of the cornerstones of the Swedish welfare state model. Since the welfare state is realised within the municipalities and the county councils, the need for trained public servants has been greatest at the local level.

Public administration in Sweden is highly decentralised. During the past two decades many tasks and responsibilities have been transferred from higher to lower levels of government, i.e. from state to local government. There has also been decentralisation within the different levels of government: from municipal council to specific policy boards, from political boards to managers, from managers to employees. One could argue that public administration has changed from being a rather exclusive task for a few to one involving very large numbers of employees at different levels, including almost all employees within state, county council and municipal administrations.

In 1997 almost 200,000 people were employed by the State and almost one million by county councils and municipalities, which is about 27 per cent of the whole working force in the country (Statskontoret,1998). The number of public employees used to be even higher but the deteriorating public finances during the 1990s have forced both local and central government to decrease employment. Women constitute a large proportion of the labour force. The majority of women are employed by county councils (80 per cent) and the municipalities (74 per cent). More than half of the women work only part-time. In the State administration 43 per cent are women (Statistiska Meddelanden).

With only a few exceptions chief executives are hired and none are elected. The few political appointments comprise Under-Secretaries of State, Press Secretaries and political advisers, all within the ministries. This means that changes in political majority within local, regional and central governments do not change the management in public administration.

Public Administration in Sweden used to be a textbook example of the Weberian tradition, especially when it comes to the loyalty of public servants, but also regarding the structure of the organisation and the application of rules. However, decentralisation has changed much of the way both employees and authorities act and organise. Due to a higher level of education among the public, citizens in general today put more pressure on public authorities and public servants.

Internationalisation means that public servants today are to some degree exposed to different administrative cultures and traditions. The Nordic countries have a mutual agreement since 1977 on cross-border co-operation between local and regional authorities (DS 1994:67) Municipalities, country councils and county administrative boards provide services or give access to public establishments for citizens on both sides of the border. Authorities co-operate in health care, primary education, rescue services, sewage treatment works etc. Patients may choose a doctor and school on the other side of the border if it is closer to home. This type of co-operation requires good knowledge of the other country's administrative system, and in some cases also language skills.

Development of Public Administration as an Academic Discipline

Public Administration programmes in Sweden have developed along two lines. Firstly, at the universities there have long been programmes targeted towards employment within the civil service. The main emphasis used to be on law and later on politics. Parts of these programmes gradually merged into one, training students within the general field of Public Administration.

Secondly, there are those Public Administration programmes directed at local officials. In the beginning it was the development of the welfare state that made programmes for local officials important. An Institute for Social Work was established in 1920 in Stockholm by the city of Stockholm and The Association for Social Work (Socialhögskolan, 1981). Since the welfare state is mainly delivered at the local level in Sweden, the need of trained officials was greatest in the municipalities.

During the first years the number of students at the Institute was rather low, partly because of difficulties in attracting students. The programme started initially with 30 students per year and by 1939/40 the number of students enrolled had increased to 100 a year (Gustafsson et al, 1986). Teachers involved usually had an academic degree or practical experience from the field of social work. Some of the teaching staff had full-time positions, others who came from the universities were engaged on an hourly basis. The programme was two and a half years in length with an 8-month internship. Students graduated as Trained Social Workers.

A few years later, in 1944, a second institute was established in Göteborg and three years later a third one in Lund. The institutes were partly financed by the government and partly by the municipalities. In 1960 the government stated that it was necessary to reorganise the programme. A Royal Commission was set up, and one of its subsequent recommendations was the establishment of an institute in Umeå (Ecklesiastikdepartementet, 1963).

Three different programmes were established at the Social Work institutes (Socialhögskolan, 1981). One was aimed at training social workers, a second at local officials employed by the municipalities, and the third was a general social science programme. In the 1950s, when there was a wave of municipal amalgamations, it was decided that there was a need for a fourth programme to train officials in fiscal matters. These latter students were supposed to obtain employment in the bigger municipalities, whereas students on the other programmes were intended for the smaller municipalities. During this period some of the municipalities employed only one official and this person clearly required broad training in order to be able to take care of all matters in the municipality.

Gradually the requirements were increased regarding the educational background of persons working within public administration as with the further development of the welfare state it became obvious that the municipalities needed more trained officials.

In the 1960s a university based Public Administration programme was introduced at the Universities of Stockholm, Göteborg, Lund and Umeå and at the University College of Östersund. Students had the opportunity to take some optional courses but in the main the major subjects were political science, economics, statistics, and social and economic geography with a special focus on Public Administration. A second wave of municipal amalgamations occurred in the late 1960s and early 1970s. The number of municipalities was reduced to 278. The effect was an increase in the number of employees, which further increased the demand of well-trained local officials.

Public Administration programmes at the institutes were from the beginning targeted mainly towards the local level. However, in 1974 a new Public Administration programme (*Linjen för offentlig förvaltning*) was introduced at a number of universities. Students were expected to be employed mainly by State authorities after graduation. The core subjects were politics and economics. In 1977 higher education in Sweden underwent a reform which resulted in the instituted of social work being incorporated with universities. The main reason for this was to strengthen links between higher education and research. The programmes did not, however, change much regarding content.

The next higher education reform came only a few years later. In the beginning of the 1980s it was discovered that the number of educational programmes had increased and that many programmes overlapped regarding content (Gustafsson et al, 1986). Some of the programmes included internship, others not, some had a more theoretical approach, others were more practically oriented. A committee was set up by the National Board for Higher Education consisting of university teachers and professors, representatives of higher education authorities and the Association for Local Authorities. The chairman was the professor in political science in Umeå. The group suggested that a new Public Administration programme should be introduced. It would consist of basic studies for one and a half years and after that the students could choose between two alternatives: one in Public Administration and the other in economics.

The latest changes in Public Administration programmes were undertaken at the beginning of the 1990s. Some universities moved away from an integrated to one which focused more on the core subjects, often mixing Public Administration students with those graduating in political science, economics, statistics etc. One explanation for this is that a new budgetary system was introduced in higher education forcing university departments into large-scale production.

Democracy, Rule of Law and Efficiency - the Holy Trinity in Swedish Public Administration

Public Administration, in a broad sense, can be divided into rule of law (the discipline of law), rationality, efficiency and efficacy (management), and political democracy and public ethics (political science). In this trinity political science plays a major part since political democracy and public ethics are exclusive to the public sector. Management values, on the other hand, are present in all parts of society, i.e. public, private and voluntary sectors

There is a belief that the public servant does not serve democracy well unless he or she also fulfils the high demands of rule of law and efficacy. On the other hand there seems to be a dimension of conflict between the three values. The task of a public authority is to implement political decision-making. Public administration is expected to be predictable, to treat citizens equally, to be efficient and handle public resources carefully, and to act according to ethical rules. This in turn makes public administration difficult to steer and control.

As mentioned above, local governments and county councils provide the bulk of the public services in Sweden. Since both types of authorities exercise a high degree of self-government, and have elected councils that in turn appoint members of different boards, democratic aspects of public administration are highly relevant. It is essential that the future public servant understands his/her position in public administration, i.e. the concept of being a 'public servant' in a democratic society. This may, of course, vary depending on what type of policy area is involved and also on the educational background of the public servant. Policy areas where a high degree of expert knowledge is essential tend to leave politicians in the hands of the public servants, for example in areas like environmental health. In other areas, such as culture and recreational activities, it is often the other way around or at least the influence of public officials is less.

Some of the recent reforms aim at increasing the possibilities for citizens to influence both politics and administration. One example is neighbourhood governments, which were introduced during the 1970s and 1980s. The original objective was to increase democracy, but gradually efficiency came into focus. Neighbourhood governments have an administration of their own. Recently the major cities have introduced these bodies: Stockholm, Gothenburg and Malmö. Other reforms aim at reducing the public sector by contracting out and by turning over responsibilities for programmes to co-operatives and voluntary non-profit organisations.

It has become increasingly popular to turn day care centres, schools, recreation centres etc into profit centres. In some cases different activities are placed under joint management in order to cut costs. Yet another example is so called citizens' advisory bureaux, municipal offices that provide all kinds of services for citizens. The idea is to simplify contacts with the bureaucracy for ordinary people. New methods in allocating money, monitoring performance, the introduction of purchaser-provider models, goal-steering techniques have also changed the way the bureaucracy works. Combined with an on-going decentralisation this means a greater freedom of action both at lower levels of government and for public officials. It is important for higher education to provide students with the proper skills in order for them to meet the demands of modern public administration. Public administration today embraces many different features. Thus, the programmes offered need to have a high degree of options available to students.

Public Administration Programmes Today

Public Administration programmes are taught at 10 universities and university colleges (Göteborg, Karlstad, Linköping, Lund, Stockholm, Sundsvall, Växsjö, Örebro, Östersund, Umeå), all in the faculties of Social Sciences. Students graduate as *Politices kandidat* (BA degree) or *Politices magister* (MA degree). The studies take three or four years respectively. In a few cases only the former degree is available, and in one case only the latter. Most students graduate as *Politices magister*.

Admission to Public Administration programmes is centralised through the National Admissions Office to Higher Education. The general entry requirements are completed secondary school *or* adult secondary school *or* folk high school *or* 25 years of age plus four years of working experience *or* foreign secondary school of minimum 12 years. In addition a certain level of Swedish, English, civics and mathematics are required (specific requirements).

Swedish Public Administration programmes were originally established on an interdisciplinary basis, in the sense that there was close co-operation between the subjects involved. The students had several different subjects during one semester, combining for example, courses in political science, economics, statistics and law. Since 1993/94 they have been organised differently. Students only take one subject per semester. This is also common in other academic disciplines. In Sweden students study one subject per semester and one course at a time. One academic semester comprises 20 credits (30 ECTS credits). One Swedish credit corresponds to one week's full-time studies, which for students mean approximately 40 hours per week including lectures and seminars. However, the students plan their own time for reading, writing, individual and group assignments etc. Most undergraduate programmes require a minimum of six semesters or three years. The Bachelors degree comprises 120 credits (180 ECTS credits) of which 60 credits should be taken in one major subject. The Masters degree comprises 160 credits (240 ECTS credits) with at least 80 credits in the major subject.

The Swedish higher education system is highly decentralised. This means that the contents of every Public Administration programme is formally decided upon by the Social Science Faculty at each university. Every department involved in the programme also has a high degree of freedom when it comes to the contents of courses, although planning and negotiations are undertaken within the boards - consisting of representatives of all teaching departments involved - for Public Administration programmes. The main impression is that the programme planning is conducted in an atmosphere of mutual interest and consensus.

Apart from the basic courses, which are usually compulsory, Swedish Public Administration programmes usually consist of a number of options for the students. The freedom of choice is also considerable when one compares the universities within the country. It is therefore impossible to describe one Swedish programme, or even one programme at one university. The only common denominator seems to be studies in politics and economics. In the majority of programmes students are allowed considerable choice of options. Although special emphasis is placed on the public sector, the students are trained for employment in both public and private sectors as well as the voluntary sector.

In most programmes courses are not exclusively for Public Administration students, especially at the more basic levels. One clear exception is Göteborg where there is no co-ordination between programme courses and single-subject courses. At some universities and university colleges a set of courses are provided only for Public Administration students. These courses are usually at intermediate and advanced levels.

All Swedish Public Administration programmes, except in Göteborg, include basic studies in political science, such as political theory and international relations. The common core at the basic level consists of both Swedish politics and administration and comparative studies. Even if the word *administration* is not mentioned in the title of a course, the aspect may be dealt with anyway. There is usually at least one book on the reading list covering the subject in some political science courses.

Public Administration programmes today deal less with traditional administrative tasks like how to construct a budget or write policy proposals. Instead they focus on the broader environment where Public Administration acts, actors involved etc. New Public Management, evaluation, implementation, European studies and gender issues are among the themes that have become popular during the 1990s. Courses on the European Union as a politico-administrative system are the most common. Lund offers 'Negotiations and Decision Making in the European Union', Sundsvall 'European Integration', and Göteborg 'Policy Making in the European Union', just to mention a few. All programmes have at least one course dealing with comparative perspectives.

Teaching methods vary quite widely. Apart from lectures and seminars, students have individual and group assignments. Case methods and problem-based learning are increasingly popular. Elements regarded as very important in Swedish higher education are the minor, senior and Masters theses, which are required by law.

The balance between theory and practice has changed over the years. In the beginning practice was emphasised, today theoretical aspects are more important. In most programmes internship is available as an option, in Sweden or abroad. Internship abroad may be at Swedish authorities like embassies. In one programme internship abroad is compulsory. Another way of providing practical perspectives is to invite public servants as guest lecturers.

The growing internationalisation in higher education plays an important part for Public Administration students. Studies abroad for one or two semesters are possible in most programmes. Students go out either within an exchange agreement or as free movers, mostly to Western countries. During their stay abroad they can learn about foreign public administration both by taking courses in the subject and by living in another country experiencing everyday contacts that citizens have with public authorities.

Within Europe the SOCRATES programme, financed by the European Commission, also invites universities to exchange teachers and to develop joint courses. The reason for introducing teacher exchange is that only a small percentage of students will ever have an opportunity to study abroad. By exchanging teachers most students will get in touch with teachers from other countries and experience different types of teaching methods. Visiting scholars in the field of Public Administration increase knowledge about different systems and also about specific perspectives on Public

Administration.

Joint course development also brings teachers and researchers from different countries together. The objective is to create a course or a core for a course to be offered at all universities taking part in the project. One example of interest from a Public Administration point of view is 'Local and Regional Government in Europe', co-ordinated by the author. This two year project aims at creating a core curriculum for a course called 'Sub-National Governments in Europe'. Participants are twelve universities from ten countries. The new course will be offered at most of the participating universities during the academic year 1998-99.

The group is also working on a textbook, which consists of articles on different aspects of Public Administration, such as democracy, regionalisation, local government etc. Members of the group are encouraged to share research and teaching material in order to enhance the comparative perspective in the articles.

Experiences from the project are so far very positive. Apart from exchanging information and knowledge on Public Administration the group has learned a lot about both their own and other European higher education systems.

Public Administration and Management Training

In Sweden, as elsewhere in the world, it has gradually become obvious that university education is not sufficient once and for all. In recent years there has been a growing demand for courses and programmes for public servants at all levels. One well established programme is that in health care administration for nurses and health care administrators. This programme has been offered at several universities, mostly as a part-time programme. Departments involved are usually political science, economics, sociology and sometimes also law.

Many of the new courses/programmes that have been introduced during the 1990s aim at middle and senior public servants. In some cases courses are part of regular university programmes, in other instances public authorities purchase specific courses and programmes. There is a development council for state authorities *(Utvecklingsrådet för den statliga sektorn)* that has purchased a whole MA programme in Public Administration from some universities. The students are civil servants in management positions and usually with a BA degree in Public

Administration. In one of the programmes, which started in 1999, the Department of Sociology in Lund and the Department of Political Science in Umeå share responsibility. This programme is particularly interesting because one of the courses is going to take place at Leeds University in Great Britain with British lecturers and tutors. Some universities also offer a Masters programme for civil servants and local officials, for example in Umeå. The entry requirements are a BA degree and a minimum of two years as a middle manager in public administration. This is a part time programme consisting of both special courses and regular courses at advanced level.

Other programmes designed to meet particular needs include policy analysis, evaluation, steering models, decentralisation, gender issues and the meaning of internationalisation. Courses concerned with the European Union and Europe are always in high demand. Since most of the course participants only have a BA degree, many programmes are at Masters level. Teaching methods drawing on the know-how of the participants are favoured. Assignments including the Masters thesis often have a connection with the authority where the participant is employed. It is, however, obvious that this may create a problem in the sense that the observer also may be part of the observed phenomena. On the other hand there are some positive effects as well. The student has good knowledge about matters related to the object of study and the employer often also gains something.

Much vocational training, however, is provided by employers and takes place in-house. In some cases there is a close co-operation with universities, in others there is none. Such training includes everything from regular courses to one-day meetings with hired lecturers.

New Challenges

Swedish Public Administration programmes seem to be well regarded by employers because most students are employed soon after graduation. In the early 1990s some 90 per cent found relevant employment within six months of finishing the programme. The picture has remained consistent despite recent cutbacks in public sector employment. There is a growing job market within the voluntary sector, and the private sector has also discovered the qualifications students get in the programmes.

By tradition Public Administration programmes are developed in line with changes within the welfare state and public administration as a whole. There has always been a close interplay between the providers of education and public employees when programmes have been discussed and planned. However, a number of new challenges are now evident. Western influences in public administration, mainly from the Anglo-American sphere, are obvious. A recent Royal Commission states that Sweden has a lot to learn both from EU and OECD countries (SOU, 1997). The introduction of ICT means changes in ways of working. All levels of government are using ICT extensively, both internally as an instrument for administrative tasks and externally for information and other purposes. Electronic services are also being developed, and 'self-service' is being introduced to a larger extent. As stated in a recent report, 'without IT, central-government – and therefore the whole of society – would grind to a halt' (Statskontoret, 1998).

University teachers are also challenged. One way of learning about developments within public administration is through research projects. Another way is by taking on assignments, for example evaluations within public administration. Governments at all levels have a tradition of purchasing evaluations/research from the universities.

The present challenges for Swedish public administration are to be found in the fragmentation of public administration and in the effects of internationalisation, especially since Sweden joined the European Union. There has also been a slight shift from public administration towards public management. Efficiency is emphasised on behalf of democratic and legal aspects, but on the whole the balance between the three still remains. It is the task of elected politicians to decide if this will be the case in the future as well, but some responsibility falls on the public servants, and, in the end, on the providers of training and education in Public Administration.

References

DS (1994), 67. *Gränssamarbete i utveckling*. Stockholm, Fritzes. (Developing Cross-Border Co-operation. Report by the Committee on Cross-Border Co-operation).

Ecklesiastikdepartementet (1963), 10. *Högre utbildning och forskning i Umeå II*. Huvudbetänkande av 1962 års Umeåkommitté.

Gustafsson, E. et al, (1986), *Förvaltningssocionomer från Umeå Universitet - en studie av examinerade socionomer mellan åren 1968 och 1982*. Umeå Universitet: Enheten för förvaltningsutbilning. FEXU-projektet.

Häggroth, S. et al, (1993), *Swedish Local Government. Traditions and Reforms*, The Swedish Institute, Stockholm.

Petersson, O . (1994), *Swedish Politics*, Publica, Stockholm.

Socialhögskolan 60 år (1981), *Institutionen för socionomutbildning/Socialhögskolan*, Stockholms universitet, Stockholm.

SOU (1997), 57. *I medborgarnas tjänst. En samlad förvaltningspolitik för staten. Betänkande av Förvaltningspolitiska kommissionen*. Stockholm, Fritzes. (Serving the Citizen. Report by the Public Administration Commission).

Statistiska Meddelanden Am 50 SM 9801, Am 51 SM 9301, Am 52 SM 9801. Statistiska Centralbyrån. (Statistics Sweden).

Statskontoret (1998), 5. *Staten i omvandling 1998*. Stockholm, Statskontoret. (The Swedish Central Government in Transition, 1998. The report includes a summary in English).

UHÄ-rapport 1978:II, 'Administrativ och ekonomisk utbildning i framtiden. En diskussionspromemoria från AU-gruppen', UHÄ, Stockholm.

UNDP, *Human Development Report 1998*, Oxford University Press, New York.

9 Starting from Nothing: Public Administration Education and Training in Ukraine

ANATOLII OLEKSIENKO

Introduction

At the end of the 20th century Ukraine emerged in the world as a new independent state known more by its nuclear missiles and the Chernobyl catastrophe than for its rich historical and cultural heritage. The Ukrainian picture looked to be deteriorating. Despite good natural resources and good skills Ukraine was running into higher debts and demanding more and more aid from abroad whilst the pace of reforms within the country continued to slow down. Ukraine's poor image confirmed that the country was struggling with tremendous developmental challenges. One could also argue that gaining independence was difficult at a time when globalisation seemed to indicate increasing interdependence.

The leading nations found it difficult to deal with a world which was no longer divided into distinct spheres and Ukraine has had to make tremendous efforts simply to prove that it was not Russia any more, nor ever was.

Historically Ukraine has had a European orientation, and from the moment of independence, Ukraine has tried to find the correct language to take part in a common Europe. The alternative, a nation with nuclear weapons, squeezed between NATO and Russia, would not satisfy Ukrainian citizens who desired the consumer products of the West.

Building a New State

In 1991 when Ukraine obtained independence many expected that reforms would sweep through the Ukrainian Parliament and Cabinet of Ministers. Some Western commentators believed that freed from Russia, Ukraine would enjoy a new prosperity. These forecasts proved to be far too optimistic; the country did not start to move faster – it halted and viewed with suspicion the struggles of other former Communist partners as they struggled with the unknowns of the market environment.

Later Ukraine would rush to catch up but found the country catastrophically lagging behind. In part due to poor administration, attempts to bring change and start a market economy in the Ukraine proved futile. Old mechanisms and structure broke but new ones often failed to begin. As an economist noted at the time, the ship was ready to go, the captain vigorously turned the wheel, but the engines would not start.

In many ways the Ukrainian bureaucracy turned out to be a broken engine. Bureaucrats were impotent in attempting to manage the changes and as a result the country actually began to go backwards. For example, whilst bureaucrats changed their colours, laws such as that implementing the Ukrainian language in public agencies were ignored to the extent that it made the Ukranianisation policies of the Soviet Union in the 1920s look like a tremendous success.

The situation could be partly explained by the fact that the majority of specialists in government opted to leave their jobs to accept positions in the private sector as a result of the new market opportunities. Those left in the bureaucracy were more efficient in 'Leninist' practice than in efficient management and administration.

The legacy of the former Soviet system of administration has seriously hindered the reform process. For a long time the brain drain from Kiev to Moscow devastated the Ukrainian bureaucracy. A mandate to work in Moscow was considered a promotion under the Soviet system. The Ukrainian bureaucracy has therefore had no incentive to cultivate national consciousness and the few attempt made were unsuccessful.

At the same time the reputation of the bureaucracy continued to fall, making employment in the public sector unattractive. The bureaucracy was seen as a burden on the state budget and was openly mocked by its marginal dependants, pensioners, teachers and students. However, some experts in the field argue that the number of civil servants was relatively low and that there were insufficient human resources in the Ukrainian civil service and in the wider management and implementation of policy.

Bohdan Krawchenko (1985), Director General of the Institute of Public Administration and Local Government, Cabinet of Ministers of Ukraine noted:

> In a society where everyone formerly worked for the state, everyone [believed that we had] a monstrous bureaucracy. This is absolutely not the case...

Ukraine has a population of 53 million, it has the territory of France. The entire public service in the Ukraine – central, regional, local, municipal, village is 428,000 ..... The central government and all of its ministries ..... the grand total is 12,400 people. So you have a situation where more people probably work for the city of Ottawa than do in public administration in Ukraine.

Nevertheless, the strongly bureaucratic inflexible government structure left from the former USSR became a tremendous obstacle to reform. The huge number of ministries, state committees and public agencies duplicated functions and did not share their responsibilities.

At the same time those working in the bureaucracy were hardly aware of new methods of administration. Bureaucrats never expected that they would have to be working to meet the demands and needs of citizens or even customers. As a result much of the market economy language was little more than empty words. Used for public speeches these words meant little to the policy making process and later became discredited in public opinion

A further factor is that the Ukrainian government has had to create new ministries (eg Foreign Affairs, Defence, Central Bank) taking over from the former responsibilities of Moscow. The new structures required new expertise and modern skills of administration. Some of these new ministries started life with three to five people working in them.

The unpredictability and incompetence of the Ukrainian bureaucracy became even more evident with the development of international businesses in Ukraine. It was clear that civil servants had neither the skills nor the orientation to cope with the new environment and in many cases demonstrated an inclination towards corruption. The ministries became political battlefields for two groups; namely, Communist-oriented and democratic groups. Very often this resulted in no action being taken at all.

The matter might have been resolved more easily had there been a tradition of allocating power amongst two or three competing political parties. Instead the Ukrainian Parliament was divided between at least twenty parities with the democratic wing, for example, made up of ten differing parties. A common Ukrainian saying is that where there are three Ukrainians there are two presidents. The legislature has succeeded in increasing the unpredictability and instability of the bureaucracy and blurring its responsibility.

Regarding presidential power, the first Ukrainian President was often criticised for preferring the status of a British monarch. However with no rights to implement policy he had very few options open to him but to try and be effective in international politics. The second Ukrainian President changed this and oriented his role towards domestic issues. This was difficult because of the lack of clarity about the division of powers. He did, however , manage to find compromises and urged the Ukraine Parliament to sign a Constitutional Agreement that specified responsibilities and rights to be shared between President and Parliament. Unfortunately the role and power of the judiciary remained poorly defined and hence conflicts between the branches continued to threaten the stability of administration.

Nevertheless the Constitutional Agreement finally specified that the central executive organs had to control their local offices which previously had been accountable to the legislative organs. Thus a new bureaucratic system began to take shape. The President also created a Control and Monitoring Committee to supervise how and when issued decisions were to be implemented.

At the same time the Law on the Civil Service was taken up by the Civil Service Commission who used it to become the organisation responsible for career development and structures in the new public bodies. The Law on the Civil Service had been well written, drawing upon the best international experience. It defined the civil service in Ukraine as being an unbiased service, permeated with selflessness, integrity, accountability, objectivity, honesty and leadership. The Law specified that recruitment to, and promotion within, the civil service will be on a merit basis. All civil servants were put into a hierarchy of fifteen ranks and five categories. Thus career prospects were clarified.

The First Institution of Public Administration Training in Ukraine

From its early days the Ukrainian State desperately felt the shortage of properly trained policy makers and mangers. The idea for creating a modern civil service training system in Ukraine was promoted by two prominent academics of Ukrainian origin – Dr Bhodan Krawchenko, Director of the Canadian Institute of Ukrainian Studies, University of Alberta and Dr Bhodan Havrylyshyn, Director of the International Management Institute, Geneva. They were convinced that Ukraine could become an advanced country provided that it had a developed bureaucracy. Being at the head of the Council of Advisers to the Parliament of Ukraine they could bring their experience and influence to the Ukrainian government.

The idea for the establishment of the Institute of Public Administration originated in discussions of the Councils of Advisers to the Ukrainian

Parliament in 1991. It was obvious that the training of civil servants was an essential step in establishing a democratic society based on the rule of law.

As one of the founders noted, on 18th December Bohdhan Krawchenko wrote a proposal to the presidium of the Parliament urging the creation of the Institute of Public Administration. At the end of 1991 a four person delegation from the President's administration visited France, including a visit to the Ecole Nationale d'Administration. Throughout early 1992 the idea of an institute was then discussed in various state bodies.

On 4th March 1992 President Kavchuk issued a decree creating the Institute of Public Administration. The Institute was to conduct research on the theory and practice of public administration, local and regional government, train personnel for organs of state administration, local and regional government and train the leading personnel of state enterprises.

The decree instructed the Cabinet of Ministers to ratify statutes of the Institute, provide appropriate facilities, appoint the management of the Institute and determine the student selection process.

Six months later the Institute enrolled its first 100 students for a one-year MPA programme. Entry was allocated with 80 places for civil servants and 20 representatives from the public at large. It was declared that at least 20 per cent of the students should be women, thus establishing East and Central Europe's first affirmative action programme. All entrants were required to have completed a course of higher education and normally to be under 40 years of age. Selection to the Institute was on a competitive basis with entrance and examination procedures ensuring strict anonymity. Students had three examinations, one written examination on the history of the Ukraine, one written examination which tested the ability to interpret data and draw conclusions, and finally an oral examination dealing with public administration in the Ukraine. Students were ranked according to their scores with the top 100 being offered places.

The list of students offered a place was subject to Cabinet of Ministers ratification. This procedure is essential to obtain stipends and a government commitment to then employ the graduates. By 1995 over 600 students were applying for the 100 places.

During the early years of the Institute a wide range of training programmes in administration and management were developed. There were nine specific developments:

- The Master in Public Administration, validated by the University of North London. The programme offers full time training for those intending to occupy middle or senior ranking posts.
- Short-term executive development posts through the Institute's centre for continuing development.
- To enhance the training of appointed and elected public officials in regional and local governments, a branch was established in Dnipropetrovsk – a major industrial centre in Eastern Ukraine. The branch offers a Masters programme and short term courses.
- The International Centre for Policy Studies was established as a partnership between the Open Society Institute, Budapest and the Institute.
- Training of managers of state enterprises is conducted through the International Centre for Privatisation, Investment and Management. This is a partnership between the Central European University (supported by the Soros Foundation) and the Institute.
- Special training in economic and finance and in economic policy for government officials – a high priority in Ukraine – is conducted through the World Bank, Economic Development Institute and the Institute's training centre.
- Training of personnel in banking is conducted through a Bank Training Centre of which the Association of Commercial Banks, the National Bank of Ukraine and the Institute are founders.
- A Masters in Health Administration degree, developed with the assistance of the World Bank mission.
- A Women's Executive Development Programme supported by the Canadian Centre for Management Development, training Ukrainian women in leadership skills.

Although many of these programmes shared resources with the Institute, only the MPA and the short-term courses were directly controlled by the Institute.

Working in a difficult environment required Institute directors to often seek support within official circles. Special attention was given to gaining approval from the Cabinet of Ministers. The senior management team reported to a Board of Directors whose membership included the Deputy Prime Minister as chairman, two representatives from Parliament, three from the Cabinet of Ministers, two leading Ukrainian scholars and five western specialists. The Board however gave the Institute full autonomy in deciding questions of academic content.

The Academic Council of the Institute was the highest academic authority of the Institute. It was responsible for the academic quality of the MPA, providing procedures to review, monitor and approve courses within the programme. The Council met at least four times a year to approve decisions and discuss major strategy issues.

Everyday management was the responsibility of a co-ordinators' council which met to ensure consistency and co-operation within the Institute. The first graduates created a council, which has played an important role in supporting former students in the workplace, where they have often met with some resistance. This Alumni Association has held an annual conference where papers on the Ukrainian Civil Service are presented. The Association also has a professional magazine, which provides an important medium for discussing economic and political reform.

Problems with Starting a Discipline of Public Administration in Ukraine

It was tremendously difficult to begin training and research in Public Administration. The subject had never been considered as suitable in the Soviet Union. Communist declarations emphasised that power belonged to the people and that the Soviet people entrusted power to the Communist Party. The Lenin postulate that a housewife could easily run the state led to a belief that no special training was required to succeed in administration. As a result most of the early Soviet elite was often poorly educated. Political masters often required little professionalism, not even obedience to Marxism-Leninism, but rather obedience to the leadership, i.e. to the Communist Party.

Later, with educational and technological developments, the higher echelons were required to become more sophisticated in their interpretation and promotion of Soviet ideology. Thus a Higher Party School was opened and became the threshold for entering the higher class of the Communist administration.

Later in his life Lenin revised his attitude towards the bureaucracy. For many years the bureaucrat had served as a scapegoat for policy failures and became a familiar satirical figure. In the 1970s and 1980s, however, although the word 'bureaucrat' remained a derogatory phrase, public service ceased to be an area of criticism as it was totally under the control of the Communist Party. Most civil servants were, out of necessity, party members, and implemented policy unquestioningly.

Consequently public administration was never considered appropriate for training under the Soviet system.   Instead the elements of Public Administration were supposed to be delivered through courses such as history of the Communist Party, historical materialism or the political economy of socialism, (which were obligatory in all undergraduate courses irrespective of specialisation). The only schools that might have trained in management or administration were those that belonged to the KGB or the military – as a result their specialists were the best trained for such work and were later highly valued by Ukrainian presidents.

In the civil schools the law faculties were probably the only ones which provided courses dealing with problems of state and law. There were thus a number of courses related to Public Administration but they strictly followed legal documents and the norms of the Soviet bureaucratic machine.

This history meant that for independent Ukraine the beginnings of Public Administration were significantly influenced by specialists from the Institute of State and Law who interpreted Public Administration from a legal perspective, arguing that bureaucrat should be guided only by the letter of the law. Thus when the first academics from abroad gave lectures, students could not understand why they took to philosophising so much about the way Ukrainian law did things one way and not another.

As a result studies began with neither the proper resources nor a proper understanding of the subject. In addition it was difficult to move from old 'chalk and talk' teaching methods with no attention given to directed private study. The trainers also failed to recognise the significant resource problems the Institute had in terms of books and course materials. Thus the Institute specified that visiting professors should complete their stay in the Ukraine by publishing relevant books or other publications. As a result the main textbook which took into account public administration in the Ukraine was published by Glenn Wright a visiting American Professor.

A final problem was inadequate staff resources. With no specialists within the Ukraine who had a developed understanding of public administration it was very difficult to start a course. The only option was to ask international trainers and schools of administration to provide staff to begin programmes.

Development of the MPA Programme

From the early days of the Institute a decision was taken to keep it away from the Ministry of Education. This was to keep it away from old Soviet school traditions and to ensure the Institute was kept away from bureaucrats keen to retain old methods. As a result the Institute was unique in being a stand-alone body separate from the educational system but affiliated to the Cabinet of Ministers. Significant foreign investment and support was also important as it meant that the Institute did not have to depend upon the Ministry of Education for funds.

The Institute was expected to train civil servants who would be able to effectively develop and implement policies in different spheres of public activity. At the same time it was to cultivate a philosophy of service to the common good, loyalty to the Ukrainian state, political neutrality, an understanding of the principles of the rule of law and a commitment to political democratisation, economic reform and social justice.

The MPA curriculum was developed after consultations with the staff of the Secretariat of Parliament, the Administration of the President and the Cabinet of Ministers. Intensive discussions were also held with French, German, Spanish, British, American and Canadian specialists.

The MPA programme succeeded in meeting the evaluative criteria of steering committees from Western partners. The University of North London validated the programme which contributed to the recognition of the Institute's academic success in the international training market. Validation also helped within Ukraine as it set standards which others could follow.

The early development of the MPA programme was not without difficulty. The first MPA was designed to include major courses such as Public Administration, political science, economics and finance, law and legislative processes, social policy, information technology and a thesis. In the second year a number of changes were introduced dividing courses into core and elective modules. All students had to take core modules in Public Administration and political science and then selected a number of electives. Three courses; economic and finance, law and legislative processes, and social policy offered block specialist modules. The Institute experienced a number of timetabling problems with this scheme and this required further customer-oriented development over the next years.

The Masters programme made every effort to ensure understanding of the general concepts of Public Administration and management, as well as political science. Specifically courses dealt with the basic functions of the public service, questions of democracy and bureaucracy, organisational development and behaviour, human resource management, policy and planning, leadership, communication and management of change. Attention was also given to practical skills such as office management, public relations etc.

Political science courses introduced students to comparative political economy and comparative politics. Courses also included study of the relationship between politics and economics, state and market institutions, ideologies, comparative political institutions and international relations. The material was intended to provide students with an understanding of the transition to democracy. The course also required students to take a module in the history of the Ukraine, as many students were unfamiliar with the real history of the country they were going to reform.

A number of courses were oriented towards studies in public policy making. Thus courses on economic and finance in addition to the fundamentals of market economics introduced micro and macroeconomics as well as the fundamentals of public sector finance. It also explored key policy issues, such as macroeconomic stabilisation, privatisation, liberalisation and de-monopolisation, economic restructuring and the role of the state. Students in Kiev were more oriented towards problems of the central state, those in Dnipropetrovsk considered regional issues.

As legislation was becoming a significant part of public administration in Ukraine, and ministries were complaining of a dire shortage of lawyers, the MPA programme also gave considerable attention to some branches of law, such as state law, comparative law, administrative law and legislative drafting. With the need to retrain those who completed their legal education under the Soviet systems, specialist courses covered legal principles across a wide range of topics such as civil law, company law and financial law.

To provide all students with understanding of modern trends in the development of information technologies a special course was designed to offer hands-on skills.

In discussion with international colleagues it was often observed and remarked that the Ukrainian MPA programme included some modules which traditionally were not offered in Western institutes. However, the reason for this was that many students had insufficient knowledge from their Soviet education.

All MPA students were also encouraged to study a foreign language as there was a shortage of public servants with language skills. Courses in English, German and French were offered.

At the end of the academic year, after formal academic studies, students have to undertake an internship either in the Ukraine or abroad. The objective of the internships was to verify the student's ability to adapt quickly to the new environment and provide additional practical training.

As the programme developed new courses were added. A programme on urban management was introduced following requests from local government in the big cities who had few specialists with an understanding of urban needs. Urban management was offered as a specialisation taken by mainly serving local government officials. A new approach towards urban management was based on comparative studies of European management experience in medium and large-scale cities. Modules offered included urban services, urban economics and urban finance.

Academic management also became more concerned with allowing more time for directed private study. The original modules had been based upon 'chalk and talk' but as they developed so trainers were asked to provide more time for private study. This became easier as more material was published on Ukrainian public administration. Significant pressure also came from students who wanted more time to concentrate on developing a thesis.

As academic management improved so attention began to be given to developing new methods of teaching. A group of Ukrainian trainers joined the Case project for Central and Eastern Europe organised by the Cascade Centre of the University of Washington. Three graduates of the Institute also received training in case writing and teaching. Ukrainian lecturers also improved their teaching skills through the Didactic Centre made available with the assistance of the German government.

Foreign Partners

From the outset the Institution has tried to be involved in as many international networks as possible. Thus the Institute became a member of the European Network of Training Organisations, the Network of Institutes and Schools of Public Administration of Central and Eastern Europe (NISPACEE), and a number of others which invited Institute staff to their conferences, workshops and seminars.

The Institute also concentrated on establishing firm ties with Western schools of Public Administration. Canadian, British, US, French and German governments all offered internships for students, fellowships for staff, staff to teach courses and assist with library development. The Institute's major partner, the Canadian Bureau for International Education supported management, offered students scholarships to the University of Manitoba, and provided instructors from Canada. The Bureau also supported library development and the publication of learning resources as well as the provision or equipment.

Using the British 'Know How' fund the Institute was able to establish a relationship with the University of North London who validate the MPA. This involved monitoring the academic procedures, staff development, research, teaching and learning methodology.

American lecturers, supported by the Fulbright Fellowship, the New York University and other US funds have contributed to the development of the programme as well as establishing new activity through NGOs and US foundations.

German Training schools, headed by the Academy in Bonn and co-ordinated by the Hans Zeidel foundation gave special attention to improving teaching methods and in developing the regional branch of the Institute.

A European Union TACIS project provided short-term training courses via specialist training centres such as ENA in France.

Western partners also significantly contributed to the development of the Library rapidly growing from just 500 volumes to in excess of 30,000. The Institute also developed an aggressive publishing programme with support for the Soros Foundation and other donors with the aim of developing a set of basic textbooks for what were the first Public Administration courses.

Further Developments

In May 1995 the President of Ukraine issued a decree stressing the need to strengthen and deepen the Institute's experience and civil service training. The decree resulted in the Institute being reorganised into the Academy of Public Administration affiliated to the President of the Ukraine. Staff thus faced a new period of challenge.

New regulations were introduced specifying that students had to have at least two years experience of working in the public service before entering the MPA programme. The new regulations also stipulated that selection should be by competitive examinations and should require specific knowledge in policy areas.

New teaching and academic staff arrived and it seemed that an attempt was being made to recreate a 'High Communist Party' style school. However, over a short period of time this new style was overcome by the older staff who had become familiar with Western methods of challenging leadership and open debate. Moreover, the existing programmes were safeguarded by the approval and validation documents, particularly those from the University of North London which stated that changes to the programme had to be agreed with them. Thus it can be said that attempts to politicise the Institute were averted by the early establishment of systems of validation and international support.

The challenge to the established MPA programme was further weakened due to the scale and scope of work that the new Academy was to undertake such as a new distance learning programme, further regional branches and contributions to future undergraduate programmes.

Conclusions

Ukraine has faced significant challenges during the twentieth century, particularly after achieving independence. The state was looking for a programme of reform and the civil service was expected to become a driving force in this process. The reality was that public agencies had a dire shortage of well-trained and adequately prepared bureaucrats or managers. The Ukrainian government responded by establishing its first training school in Public Administration.

The establishment of an MPA programme and a series of short courses was a difficult process. Public Administration as a subject had to take its first steps in a country where Communist ideology had for seventy years downgraded the theory and practice of administration and management. In three years the Institute managed to create an MPA programme but this was mainly due to the technical assistance of Western partners.

The Ukrainian Government has also had to learn how to pay adequate attention to the training of its public servants. However, it has been noticeable that the need for an army of skilled public managers has grown as the reform process has developed, requiring the President of Ukraine to pay far more personal attention to the preparation of civil servants.

The next stages are to continue the process by further developments within the Academy but this requires more resources and initiatives. Public Administration training and education, however, now has roots in Ukraine. The next phase will be about healthy development.

References

Krawchenko, B. (1985), *Social Change and National Consciousness in Twentieth Century Ukraine*, Canadian Institute of Ukrainian Studies, University of Alberta, Canada.
Nyzhnyk, N. (1995), 'Sotsial no-pravovyi instytut upravlinnia', *Kommandor*, nn. 1, IPALG, Kiev.
Ukraine-Canada Policy and Trade Monitor (1993), vol. 2, 1.

10 A Societal and Political Problem? Public Administration Education and Training in Venezuela

MARCO CUPOLO

Introduction

Venezuela has been a presidential democratic republic since 1958. After a military regime that ruled between 1948 and 1958, two parties, AD (*Acción Democrática*/Democratic Action) and COPEI (*Comité Politico Electoral Independiente*/Independent Political Electoral Committee), alternated in power until 1993, when Rafael Caldera, who founded COPEI but was expelled from this party in 1993, won the presidential elections leading an alliance of new parties, *Convergencia*. Previously, AD's candidate Carlos Andres Perez, the winner of the 1988 presidential elections, had implemented a radical economic readjustment (1989), stirring up a deep economic crisis and the most violent riots of contemporary Venezuelan history. In the following years, the economy grew quickly, as too did political discontent. The military attempted two coups in 1992, and Perez had to leave the presidency in 1993 because of embezzlement charges and in order to defend himself in impeachment proceedings. Ramon Velasquez was elected by Congress to serve as Acting President, but in the presidential election of December 1993 was defeated (after a partial recount) by Rafael Caldera. These recent political upheavals have been accompanied by severe economic difficulties. In 1994 much of the country's banking sector collapsed; in 1995 price increases of 20 per cent were announced. Nevertheless the country has substantial natural resources, including oil, natural gas, gold and diamonds and efforts to create a more market-oriented economy led to the IMF granting a large credit in 1996.

Venezuela's long current democratic cycle is the last stage of a rapid modernisation process triggered by financial resources resulting from oil exports. Venezuelan scholars call such financial resources *renta petrolera* (oil rent), and the link between the oil rent and politics is a key element in understanding both the expansion and the inefficiency of Venezuelan public administration. Regardless of service quality standards, the growth of public administration and public expenditure fostered by oil revenues have been crucial guarantees of political stability. The education and training of public servants, thus, has only been of secondary concern to Venezuelan governments. The current crisis, however, as well as increasing political and social demands requires better performance from public administration. While public servants' education and training should, therefore, be a priority, the Venezuelan government does not currently possess either the financial resources or the political capacity to implement a plan to meet such needs.

Public Administration and Oil Rent

In this century, before development funded by oil exports, Venezuelan public administration could not recruit particularly well qualified personnel. At that time, Venezuela was still a very traditional, rural and poor society. The demand for public services was limited and public administration, consequently, neither developed specific functions nor needed very specialised personnel. The recruitment of public servants, for example, went as follows: higher executives came from the political-economic elite, while the remaining ranks were filled by educated officials drawn from the middle class. Belonging to privileged social groups, in other words, was in itself the strongest guarantee to obtaining and keeping a job in public administration. Public servants, consequently, were not recruited on the basis of a specific area of knowledge or special qualifications or experience.

As Venezuela became an oil country, this situation began to change. First of all, following the discovery of massive oil fields between 1914 and 1917, and under the stern dictatorship of Juan Vicente Gomez (1908-1935), the country initiated a programme of political modernisation. At the same time, the growth of the oil sector prompted a demand for more competent personnel in public administration. Supervising oil companies activities, for example, needed highly qualified officials, but neither the existing pattern of recruitment to public administration, nor continuing inefficiencies within the education system, really allowed for this. As a result Venezuelan governments adjusted to what in the event became a new tradition by paying for study abroad by selected employees or individuals. For the same reason governments also began to hire special teams and experts from foreign countries to carry out specific tasks. (The Venezuelan private sector has often followed such practices, too.) The financial resources to afford such a solution, naturally, came from oil revenues. Later, the policies of democratic governments facilitated overseas study for Venezuelans from a wider section of society, especially during the oil boom of the 1970s. However, since a severe economic crisis in 1983, fewer and fewer Venezuelans have been enjoying this privilege, while government institutions have been hiring fewer, and cheaper, foreign advisers.

With modernisation, special programmes for public servants' education also started, but following a pattern characteristic of the Venezuelan education system in so far as it lacked any coherent strategy. Confusion was generated by carelessly importing different theories, methods and technologies, and also because different regimes and governments often held contrasting political views about education. Venezuelan society generally, and public administration in particular, has consequently adopted a mix of cultural patterns, study perspectives and education programmes albeit mostly from the United States. For these reasons, it is difficult to determine which, if any, specific school has been the most influential in the education of public servants. While several features of the Iberian bureaucratic tradition are still in evidence, the curriculum for Public Administration appears as the consequence of putting together heterogeneous ideas and theories from various standpoints: different foci on economics, planning, management and organisation, politics and policy, law, finance and budgeting sharing in what is supposed to be the core of the Public Administration field.

Because of the above pattern of development it is very difficult to define a Venezuelan cultural tradition in administration. The only prevailing common element is an opportunistic pragmatism, whose motto could be: 'things have to be made to work, no matter how'. The Venezuelan approach to Public Administration disciplines, thus, appears surprisingly naive, disorganised and inadequate. However, this pragmatism, through being confronted by crucial problems, has also achieved considerable goals. The best example is in several administrative sectors linked to oil where generations of very trustworthy officials have been trained by means of long running programmes. For example, since 1976, PDVSA *(Petroleos de Venezuela S.A.)*, Venezuela's state-owned oil company, has been allowed to operate as a private company, and thanks largely to its relative decision-making autonomy its efficiency stands as one of very few exceptions in the public sector. The situation in most Venezuelan public enterprises and public administration, however, is the opposite of this. For example, the Ministry of Energy and Mines, although it has obvious links with the oil sector, enjoys nothing like the same reputation for efficiency.

The Public Administration Framework

Venezuela is a federal republic consisting of 22 states, the Federal District and 72 islands. Central administration consists of the ministries and the Presidency's central offices. Numerous associations, foundations, autonomous institutes, and local administration provides decentralised administration. In accordance with the decentralisation process operating in recent years, local public administration is being granted more responsibilities and administrative tasks within the political system. However, as this change is still being implemented many sectors cannot be clearly classified either into central or decentralised administration. In any event, the financial dependence of most local administration sectors on central administration highlights the practical limitations of this decentralisation and significantly weakens the formal autonomy of local public institutions.

The number and structure of ministries has changed throughout history. Nevertheless, ministries such as Agriculture, Defence, Education, Energy and Mines, Finance, Health, Justice, Foreign and Internal Affairs, Presidency's Secretary, Transportation and Labour have consistently held key positions in the Venezuelan political and administrative system. CORDIPLAN, *(Oficina Central de Planificación y Coordinación* / Central Planning and Co-ordination Office), the government's arm for planning, OCEI, *(Oficina Central de Estadistica e Informática* / Central Statistics and Sampling Office), which gathers and supplies data on Venezuela, and OCP *(Oficina Central de Personal* / Central Personnel Office), which supervises public personnel, are the most important central offices. Their respective directors are also entitled to ministerial status.

Thirty per cent of public servants work in the decentralised sector which consists of between 400 and 500 institutions. In terms of public expenditure similar percentages, 70 per cent and 30 per cent, are attributable to central and decentralised administrations respectively. According to OCEI data the number of Venezuelan public servants was 182,097 in 1993. There were 151,555 in 1981 rising to a peak of 229,263 in 1990 (OCP, *Informes Estadisticos,* 1981-1993).[1]

Training Public Servants: Government Institutes and Training.

Many Venezuelan public institutions organise training programmes for their personnel. FUNDACITE, *(Fundación para el Desarrollo Cientifico de la Región Occidental*/Foundation for the Scientific Development of the Western Region), for example, organises a permanent seminar to train public managers in science and technology. In addition many departments of central administration organise special programmes for their own personnel. Often the titles of these courses show a clear link with English administrative terms, frequently being called *de extension* (extension) or *de inducción* (induction). Many public enterprises and parts of central and decentralised administrations also have exchange agreements of one kind or another whereby their employees can widen their experience, with the OCP playing a major role as an intermediary in organising such events. However three public institutions play a particularly important role within the Venezuelan training system for public servants.

The ENAP (*Escuela Nacional de Administración Pública*/National School of Public Administration), created by presidential decree in June 1962, is the pioneer of Public Administration studies in the current democratic cycle. It was aimed at reforming Venezuela's bureaucracy. In the light of public sector inefficiencies the then leaders of Venezuela's democracy hoped to reform the bureaucracy by turning public administration into a professional career. The original aim was for ENAP to provide undergraduate and graduate programmes in Public Administration which would lead to the formation of a new generation of public servants.

In the event the ENAP project never really took off. As a result of democratisation, political patronage increasingly supplemented socio-economic background in the selection of public servants. Thanks to oil income governments could maintain a growing bureaucracy, and compensate for any public administration inefficiencies. Consequently, professional training remained less important than membership of privileged classes or political groups, and the ENAP, therefore, quickly lost prestige. Its name was changed to ENAHP (*Escuela Nacional de Administración Pública* / National School of Administration and Public Finance), and the range of courses offered was reduced. ENAHP is now affiliated to the Finance Ministry and grants bachelor degrees in Fiscal Sciences with specialisation in Public Finance or Income Tax. Its study programme includes courses on Tax Accounting, Port Customs, Sales Tax and Public Finance. The low standards of ENAHP's graduates, however, have been one of the obstacles in recent reform of the fiscal system. When Caldera's government created the SENIAT (*Servicio Nacional Integrado de Administración Tributario* / Integrated National Service of Fiscal Administration), a new branch of the Finance Ministry, it became clear that ENAHP graduates were insufficiently prepared to assume responsibilities in the new organisation, and once again the government resorted to hiring foreign experts.

IVEPLAN (*Instituto Venezolano de Planificación* / Venezuelan Planning Institute), was founded in 1983 and works closely with CORDIPLAN. Offering specialist courses in Public Management and Global Planning, IVEPLAN is the only public institute for graduate students whose courses are related to core Public Administration studies, although generally only public servants from the central administration or the Caracas area attend its courses. Successful students can obtain a Masters degree in planning by further study at CENDES (*Centro de Estudios del Desarrollo* / Centre for Development Studies) in the Central University of Venezuela. Most IVEPLAN teaching staff are graduate public servants whose work experience is the main source of knowledge for majors in: Information Systems, Strategic Management, Organisation Development, Productivity Management, Negotiation Strategies, Project Management, Public Policies Analysis and Human Resources Management.

Founded in 1989, the *Escuela de Gerencia Social,* (School of Social Management), is a new and small institution sponsored by the Ministry of the Family (which is essentially a social development ministry). Even though this institution has agreements with several universities, its courses do not lead to an academic degree. In the future, however, the *Escuela is* expected to grant academic degrees in social policy, which hitherto has largely been disregarded as a specialism in Venezuelan Public administration. As well as providing training courses the *Escuela* has a research centre for social programmes, a data bank on social management, advises institutions responsible for or linked to social policies, and issues publications on decentralisation, social security and social policies analysis. The *Escuela* has a special interest in small enterprises and co-operative societies supported by public financing, management in local administration and policies focused on marginal social sectors.

Also of importance to the training of public officials is a special OCP training system known as SNA (*Sistema Nacional de Adiestramiento/* National Training System). Institutions can affiliate their particular programmes to the SNA, which also develops and gives courses on subjects such as standard procedures of registration and control, the organisation of information systems, and the legal basis of public affairs. The SNA began work in 1980 as part of a strategy for the modernisation of public administration but, according to a 1983 appraisal, its financial support and teaching staff were inadequate. Financial support declined after 1980, and instructors were not equipped for teaching the specialist courses of the programme (De Peña et al, 1983). In 1992, however, the SNA was finally reformed giving more autonomy to the affiliated institutions (OCP, Julio, 1992).

As part of this 1992 SNA reform, the Carlos Andrés Perez administration tried to develop the *Plan Nacional para la Profesionalización de la Gerencia Pública,* (National Plan for Public Management Professionalism), although this failed to develop as anticipated owing to a combination of financial difficulties and political changes. According to the *Plan Nacional,* education programmes linked to public and private institutions and supported by a scholarship granting organisation, *Fundayacucho,* would have promoted a particular managerial style in the Venezuelan public administration. Now, although several programmes of the *Plan Nacional* are still working, it is extremely difficult to make any forecast about the future of education plans for public servants because of the country's political and economic situation. At the time of writing further reforms in public sector training are being considered, but definitive plans have still not been formally presented.

Universities and Non Government Institutes

The UNA (Universidad Nacional Abierta/National Open University), is the only Venezuelan academic institution specifically focusing on Public Administration at undergraduate level. The UC (Universidad de Carabobo / University of Carabobo) and the Francisco De Miranda University of Coro offer specialist courses in Public Management, sponsored by IVEPLAN. The LUZ (La Universidad del Zulia / University of Zulia) formerly had a special programme for the Analysis of Public Enterprises Management but since 1986 this programme has been developing a private managerial focus. The UCAB (Universidad Católica Andrés Bello / Andrés Bello Catholic University) is able to offer a specialised course in Public Enterprise Management through its MBA Programme, and also offers specialised courses in Labour Relations Management and Human Resources focusing on the public sector. The USB (Universidad Simón Bolivar / Simón Bolivar University) offers through its different graduate programmes in Political Science, several courses related to Public Policy, Comparative Public Administration and Planning, and Human Resources Management in Public Administration. The UCV (Central University of Venezuela), the largest public Venezuelan academic institution, has Specialisation Courses in Hospitals and Public Health Administration. Finally, the UCLA (Universidad Centro-Occidental Lisandro Alvarado/Lisandro Alvarado Central-Westem University) has a Masters Programme in Public Administration offering specialisation in Administrative Planning and Agrarian administration (Quintin, 1994; OCP, November 1992).

The IESA (Instituto de Estudios Superiores de Administración / Institute of Higher Administration Studies) is a private institution created in 1965 devoted to both public and private management. However, despite sound research into Public Administration, most IESA programmes focus on private management. Its MBA programme is the most prestigious in the country, and while its MPP (Master in Public Policy) programme enjoys a good reputation it recruit relatively few students. One reason is that its courses are extremely expensive, which means that the higher salaries generally available in the private sector make its MBA programme generally more attractive as an investment. IESA also offers numerous short programmes such as: the

Executive Programme for Public Managers, Strategic Planning, Management for Non Profit Organisations, and Local Administration Management.

Finally, the ILDIS (Instituto Latinoamericano de Investigaciones Sociales / Latin American Institute of Social Research), which is funded by the German Social Democratic Party, has an intensive course in Public Management.

From this overview of Public Administration studies in Venezuelan universities and non-government institutes, the IESA stands out for its remarkable and pioneering role in management studies. Trade union demands, coupled with radical political stances, have made it difficult to establish and maintain academic standards. In response to this Venezuelan governments have tended to foster studies abroad in some fields through generous scholarship programmes. However, the social sciences have not been among these and Public Administration, through its identification with these, has been held back. This has had a damaging effect on the development of academic programmes in Public Administration and the maintenance of academic standards necessary to underpin them. IESA, however, has managed to resist many of these pressures, both because it is a prestigious private institution, and because it has developed management and public policies studies with an approach closer to that of the US schools (including an identification with Chicagoan neo-liberalism). Today IESA has the status of an elite institute, and many of its scholars and graduate students played a leading role in the economic readjustment policies of the Perez administration.

Conclusion

One of the biggest problems of the country in both the private and public sectors is the limited decision-making capabilities of Venezuelan leadership (Naim and Piñango, 1989). The IESA graduate programmes, thus, are directly relevant to the country's training needs, especially in public management education; however, as previously mentioned the MPP programme does not have a strong demand. Moreover, IESA, being a small institution, deals only with a few research areas, generally those on which information is most readily available. Because information tends to be relatively abundant in, for example, macroeconomics and public financing, these have become the main IESA research areas related to Public Administration.

A further problem is that many public institutions neglect to issue information about their activities.[2] Government indifference in this area, with a few notable exceptions such as OCEI and CORDIPLAN, means that even those educational and training programmes which are available may not be properly marketed. One obvious implication is that even if a new school for higher studies in Public Administration was to be developed (Quintin, 1994) a different attitude would be required. Significantly, a recent World Bank study (World Bank, 1992) suggested that, in the light of the ENAP experience, a radically different approach would be required.

A significant effort to improve public servants' education and training is clearly needed in Venezuela. However, the problem is such that what is required is not simply a co-ordinated plan for public service education, but a wider readjustment involving public servants' recruitment and selection and the role of public administration within the political and economic system. The poor standards of Venezuelan education are also a factor. Because public universities take between 30 per cent and 40 per cent out of the public education budget, primary and secondary schools, consequently, are neglected and lower social sectors have less chance to enter public universities. Higher social sectors, by contrast, can afford private schools, which guarantee a better education level, and subsequently progress to university. This distortion generates an unbalanced labour market which, in turn, impacts directly on public administration. Because salaries in the middle and lower ranks of the public services are not attractive they tend to recruit disproportionately from those who have fallen behind in the educational process.

Better educated professionals, by contrast, if they choose to work in the public sector often obtain temporary positions in public administration, as government advisers for example, working on well-paid contract for specific projects. Such contracts belong to the previously discussed emergency strategy of Venezuelan governments, which was roundly criticised in the World Bank (1992) report. It allows these appointees to work at the highest levels of the salary market without any stable links with public administration as a career. It leaves the public services subject to sudden and sporadic changes in personnel, making long-term programmes difficult to manage and implement, and contributes to a culture of corruption and embezzlement.

In the area of public institutions, ENAP's history should not be repeated. IVEPLAN and the *Escuela de Gerencia Social* could be the starting point for new strategies in public servants' education. IVEPLAN, for example, gathers both weakness and strength from its teaching staff. On the one hand the choice of graduate public servants as teachers assures a direct knowledge of Venezuelan public administrative processes, which are often neglected by experts trained abroad or professors with a theoretical or macro-approach background. On the other hand such an approach tends to reinforce bureaucratic continuity through its teachers at the expense of new approaches and innovation - for example, in fields such as Research and Development which require specialised staff.. The *Escuela* is a recent and interesting attempt to improve government planning. However, for a variety of reasons there is still not a firm interest in developing studies on Public Administration in public universities. The USB Masters Programme in Political Science, for example, enrols the highest number of political science PhDs in the country, yet research in Public Administration is not common.

Considering the current financial difficulties of the Venezuelan government, a small and flexible agency or centre could co-ordinate training and educational strategies for public administration among public and private institutions. As part of a long run strategy to modernise public administration, such a centre neither has to be a publicly funded institution nor has to work through bureaucratic structures such as the OCP. The main activity of the centre would be data gathering and supplying information about available educational and training programmes for public servants. According to the demand for these studies, public and private institutions would have to plan courses and research with a specific focus on the needs of central and decentralised administrations. Without significant government support, however, it is impossible to plan any realistic strategy for nothing less than a structural readjustment of the public sector would be required. And alongside that structural readjustment would be wider considerations such as a reform of the education system. Any project for reforming Public Administration education and training in Venezuela which ignores these wider factors is unlikely to succeed.

Notes

1   OCP's reports, however, have been excluding the personnel of two public institutions in recent years. See also, Calzadilla, V. *Administración Pública,* (Documentos de Base/Proyecto Venezuela Cómpetitiva), n.14, Ediciones, IESA, p. 13.

2.   In this study, for example, it proved impossible to find an updated file about SNA activities.

Spanish Abbreviations

AD*: Acción Democrática* (Democratic Action)

CENDES: *Centro de Estudios del Desarrollo* (Centre for Development Studies)

COPEI*: Comité Politico Electoral Independiente* (Independent Political Electoral Committee)

COPRE*:   Comisión Presidencial para la Reforma del Estado* (Presidential Commission for State Reform)

CORDIPLAN: *Oficina Central de Planificación y Coordinación* (Central Planning and Co-ordination Office)

ENAP: *Escuela Nacional de Administración Pública* (National School of Public Administration)

ENAIHP: *Escuela Nacional de Administración y Hacienda Pública* (National School of Administration and Public Finance*)*

FUNDACITE: *Fundación para el Desarrollo Científico de la Región Occidental* (Foundation for the Scientific Development of the Western Region)

FUNDAYACUCHO: *Fundación Gran Mariscal de Ayacucho*

IESA*:   Instituto de Estudios Supetiores de Administración* (Institute of Higher Administration Studies)

ILDIS*: Instituto Latinoamericano de Investigaciones Sociales* (Latin American Institute of Social Research)

IVEPLAN: *Instituto Venezolano de Planificación* (Venezuelan Planning Institute)

LUZ: *La Universidad del Zulia* (University of Zulia)

OCEI: *Oficina Central de Estadistica e Informática* (Central Statistics and Sampling Office)

OCP*:   Oficina Central de Personal* (Central Personnel Office)

PDVSA*:   Petróleos de Venezuela Sociedad Anónima* (Petroleos de Venezuela S.A.)

SENIAT: *Servicio Nacional Integrado de Administración Tributario* Integrated National Service of Fiscal Administration

SNA: *Sistema Nacional de Adiestramiento* (National Training System*)*

UC: *Universidad de Carabobo* (University of Carabobo)

UCAB: *Universidad Católica Andrés Bello (*Andrés Bello Catholic University)

UCLA*: Universidad Centro-Occidental Lisandro Alvarado*

UNA*: Universidad Nacional Abierta* (National Open University*)*

USB*: Universidad Simón Bolivar* (Simón Bolivar University*)*

UCV*: Universidad Central de Venezuela* (Central University of Venezuela)

References

De Peña, M. P., Cadenas, R.I. and Escobar, G. (1983), *Evaluación del sistema nacional de adiestramiento,* Unidad de Proyectos Especiales, Pres.dencia de la República, Oficina Central de Personal, Dirección de Adiestramiento, Caracas.

Naim, M. and Piñango, R.(eds.) (1989), *El caso Venezuela: Una ilusión de armonia,* 5th edn, IESA, Caracas.

OCP (Julio 1992), *Modernización de la Función Pública,* Documento 3, *(Reorientación y normas para el Funcionamiento del Sistema Nacional de Adiestra miento),* Oficina Central de Personal de la Presidencia de la República, Caracas (mimeograph.)

OCP (November 1992), *Plan nacional de formación para la profesionalización de la gerencia pública Año 1993,* Oficina Central de Personal de la Presidencia de la República, Caracas (mimeograph).

Quintin, A. (1994), 'Proyecto de creación del Instituto de Alta Gerencia Pública,' in F.Toro, J. César, A. Quintin (eds), *Reforma de las insfituciones de gobierno (Propuestas para la modernización del ejecutivo),* COPRE, Caracas.

World Bank (1992), *Venezuela, Public Administration Study,* Draft Confidential, Report No. 8972-VE, January 21,1992.

11 Concluding Thoughts: Perspectives on Training and Education for the Public Service

MORTON R. DAVIES

In recent decades there has been an increasing volume of academic and professional writing on the place of training in the development of human resources in organisations. Most authors start from the premise that training will enhance that development provided it is based on a systematic appraisal of an organisation's training needs, adopts appropriate training methodologies, and there is a continuous process of evaluation of the impact and effects of training programmes. This evaluation needs to be focused on both the individual's and the organisation's performance, and must encompass both immediate and longer term perspectives.

Whilst needs analyses pinpoint the substantive content and particular methodologies required for specific training programmes it is instructive to consider various perceptions of the nature and objectives of training *per se*. Milkovich and Boudreau (1988) define training as 'a systematic process of changing behaviour, knowledge and/or motivation of present employees to improve the match between employee characteristics and employment requirements'. It follows that assessments of the efficacy or success of a training programme must partly be measured in terms of the individual's changes of behaviour arising from newly acquired skills, learning and attitudes as a result of the training.

In the same vein Ivanicevich and Glueck (1989) define training as 'a systematic process of altering the behaviour of employees in a direction to achieve organisational goals'. Both definitions concur that training, to be effective, must be systematic, must develop from the organisation's needs than just teaching. It is also a learning process, in which the trainee must not only inculcate knowledge but must also assimilate ideas, values and norms into his/her working practices and behaviour. As was expressed almost half a century ago, 'unless something has been learned as well as taught, there is no training ... training imparts knowledge and develops skills' (*UN Handbook of Training in the Public Service*, 1966).

There has been a widespread and ongoing debate in many professions about the distinction between education and training. At the extremes there are those who try to discuss education and training in mutually exclusive terms. Education is portrayed as the instruction provided in schools and universities, whilst training is reserved for the programmes of specialised instruction in vocational schools and institutes. The former is a preparation for life in society, the latter has a vocational purpose and is designed to enhance individuals' capacities to earn a living. Frequently such arguments come from leaders of professional associations seeking to promote the interests of, or secure the exclusivity of, a narrowly defined group of professionals.

It is particularly difficult to sustain a clear distinction between education and training in discussions of training for the public service. Partly, this is because the entry qualification for many public servants is the culmination of an education programme provided by schools and/or universities. Partly, because many overtly training programmes for public servants involve discussion of social values, norms, obligations which overlap with 'the preparation for life in society' referred to above; and partly, as has been amply illustrated in the accounts of training and education given in these two volumes, training for public servants is provided from educational institutions such as universities and institutes of technology.

The collection of essays in these two volumes reveals different responses to the issues raised earlier in this conclusion, whilst concurrently showing the different systems across the globe grappling with many problems which are similar from one country to another. In most countries there is a robust attempt to come to terms with changes in the wider social environment, sometimes referred to as globalisation, which has ushered in a whole new vocabulary involving concepts such as empowerment, privatisation, public/private mix, and clientele-centred bureaucracy. In turn this new vocabulary raises (or reflects) a new concern about the role of the state, accountability and public sector management. The dominance of the language, concepts and values of the private sector must be reconciled with the ongoing circumstances of the public sector and the place of public administrators in the making of public policy. Within this common struggle to come to terms with, or accommodate, these contemporaneous developments well established distinctions about, for example, training generalists or specialists remain. For instance, public administration training in France is still determined by an individual's performance in the competitive examination which 'opens up access to different training institutes which are in reality specialised institutes' (Supra, vol.2, ch.3). By contrast, Wilson and Dwivedi's chapter (Supra, vol.1, ch.4) suggest that the Canadian response to recent developments such as downsizing and retrenchment was to re-examine core values leading to the conclusion that all public servants must 'in all their actions, respect ministerial responsibility, human rights and freedoms, the principles of federalism and the rules of law'. This seems to be a plea for a programme of training and education with significant common elements for all cadres of public servants. These common elements reflect an ongoing commitment to a traditional set of norms and values and justify the authors' conclusion that 'plus ça change, plus c'est la même chose'. Even so, the Canadian prescription appears to have been the result of a systematic attempt by key figures to examine the core values of public administration, followed by the establishment of a dedicated task force to reconfigure the public bureaucracy.

Of greater concern for those interested in the efficacy of public service training and education programmes must be the indications that many schools and institutes offer programmes which are hardly re-appraised from one decade to the next. These often take place in circumstances in which scant attention is paid to the selection of trainees, or the utility in the workplace of the skills acquired on training programmes. For example, 'the trainees for various courses are selected without any assessment of training needs and without any plan as to how the acquired skills and knowledge will be utilised after the trainees return to their workplaces...the objectives and contents of training programmes are determined by the institutions well before the selection of trainees' (Supra, vol.1, ch.3).

The contributions in the present volumes, however, give testimony to the almost universal concern to grapple with the changes that are occurring, or have occurred, in modern public services. They also reveal the continuation of many well established approaches to the training and education of public officials. For example, the emphasis in the French public service on creating a strong *esprit de corps* persists with the *grands corps* continuing to provide the institutional basis for the prestigious careers of the elites who gain entry to the *corps* as a result of success in early training and education programmes at for example, the Ecole Nationale d'Administration (ENA) or the various Ecoles Polytechniques. The *grands corps* have traditionally dominated and continue to dominate, the administrative machinery of the French state. They are instrumental in fashioning and reforming that apparatus and play a significant role in the self management of the various professions within the public service. The *grand corps* have always enjoyed considerable autonomy and are instrumental in determining the collective strategies of civil servants, and in defending the rights of civil servants, and in demanding improvements in their positions (see Rouban, 1988).

Since 1946 there has developed in France a central policy for the organisation and development of public service careers, for the determination of the nature and contents of training programmes, working conditions and salaries. Such policies and the very existence of the *grand corps* affect the culture and the social status of the public servants, and have fostered in the senior ranks of the French public service an awareness of the need to retain an appropriate relationship with politically appointed ministers and a belief in the relative autonomy to carry out its tasks of the administrative service itself. The *grand corps* with their links to the numerous professional colleges have enhanced the sense of belonging to specialist cadres, with an almost exclusive monopoly of a specific body of knowledge and skills which form the basis of their elite status. This sophisticated set of institutional arrangements facilitate a solution to the ongoing debate about the place of specialists and generalists in the public service. However the French model should not be taken as a simple model to be copied by other systems addressing similar problems. As almost all commentators on French administration attest it is only possible to explain and understand the French system by reference to their historical development from the late eighteenth century onwards. Any adoption of these, or any other, arrangements must take cognisance of that historical legacy, the constitutional, social, political and economic environments in which the administrative system and its training agencies operate, as well as the particular norms and values that dominate the public bureaucracy.

Recent decades have witnessed a number of developments which have, or should have, affected the content and delivery of training and development programmes for public servants. Among these are (i) the appearance of information technology, (ii) the emergence of regional, supranational organisations (iii) new political governmental systems and (iv) new ideas about the role of the state, and concepts of public management.

Information Technology

A recent commentator (Silcock, 1998) opines that 'there has developed a strong connection between IT and the good management of an organisation'. Another (Hopper, 1990) claims that 'the role of IT is to help organisations solve critical business problems or to deliver new services by collecting raw data and by turning that information into knowledge'. A third (MacFarlane, 1984) argues that 'new information technologies have given organisations the opportunity to redeploy their assets and rethink their strategies'.

It is clear from the above that in the modern world an integral part of the training of any competent manager, whether in the public or the private sector, should include knowledge and understanding of the new technologies and their place within managerial systems. It is therefore all the more surprising how little overt acknowledgement of the importance of this aspect of public administration training there is in these two volumes, and how seldom specifically tilted IT modules appear in the various lists of training modules, which appear in these pages. It may well be, of course, that this aspect of managerial training is imparted in other modules; but equally it may be that there remains a significant lag between the developments in management practice and what it is offered in training institutions. The limitations of time and space no doubt prevented detailed pictures of training provisions in this area from emerging.

A related issue, which found no place in most of the discussions, was that of how to satisfy the training needs of different cadre of trainee. This is a generic problem in all general management training programmes, especially in relation to the range of skills and techniques used for calculation and control within organisations. Technicians and middle managers will need to know and understand how to execute technical processes. Senior managers, close to the policy-making function, however, need to be aware of the use to which a whole range of these techniques can be put in making policies. For example, they will need to know the limitations or obligations imposed by the law without themselves being lawyers; the value of involving the workforce or the public without themselves being personnel officers or public relations specialists, the technical parameters imposed by building regulations without themselves being civil engineers etc. The dilemma for the training institution is how to devise a programme which has the right balance between technical skills and generic management training.

Emergence of Supra-national Organisations

In recent decades there has been a proliferation of regional, supra-national organisations in almost all parts of the world. For example, the European Union, the North American Free Trade Association, the Organisation of African Unity, the South East Asian Trade Association. Each of these organisations works in different ways involving their members in different obligations and different relationships. In every case, however, they involve national administrators having contact with their counterparts from other countries and those in the supra-national organisation itself. In these regional organisations where common policies and norms are being developed this is likely to involve managers in new practices within hitherto unfamiliar regulatory frameworks. Moreover these supra-national organisations which are staffed by nominees and/or secondees from member states will develop procedures which are likely to involve an amalgam of practices from those member states.

In time the development of these supra-national entities are likely to have an increasing influence on the member states, which in turn will affect the training needs in those member states. In the European context some recognition of what this involves has already appeared. Greenwood et al (Supra, vol.2, Foreword), for example, quote a recent British government report which emphasises 'that understanding of the European frameworks in which UK operates and a facility to work effectively within European institutions' is crucial to the training and development of civil servants.

Testimony that this aspect of training is already taking root and that significant benefits accrue is provided by Ziller (1993), 'Training in the European dimension has proved a powerful factor for change because administrators have been confronted by the varied cultures of their foreign counterparts. The legalistic approach of German civil servants rubs shoulders with French *esprit de corps* and the British traditions of teamwork.'

Transition to new political / governmental systems

A number of the reports in the two volumes analyse the specific problems of training in circumstances of transition. Some dealt with the immediate post-colonial period of the 1960s and 1970s; others, more contemporaneously, considered the problem in post-communist Eastern Europe, or post-Apartheid South Africa. Training, in these societies, involves, not merely instruction in the knowledge and skills of administrative processes, but requires the inculcation of a whole new set of norms and values characterising the new system of government. It requires often a complete reconsideration of the administrators' roles and relationships; a change of behavioural norms, a redefinition of goals and objectives. This is an onerous additional dimension that cannot be ignored.

It is clear from the various contributors that different approaches have been adopted in different societies. Some have focused their training resources on a relatively small group of key personnel e.g. The National School of Public Administration in Poland admits only 60 trainees a year to its postgraduate programme. By contrast the Malaysian strategy was to train as many public servants as possible e.g. in the 1970s approximately 6,000 trainees were admitted to INTAN each year. This involved training for a number of employees equal to the annual growth rate of the federal and state bureaucracies in Malaysia plus the annual replacement rate. Another feature of this group of transitional societies is the consistent practice of sending officials overseas for training. This would appear to be a convenient way of exposing trainees to new systems, ideas, values and norms of administrative behaviour whilst securing instruction in the conventional knowledge and skills in well established training institutions.

A further development is reflected in the contribution from Ukraine, where the common theme of dependence upon external sources is clear when reviewing their programmes. The influence of many modern aspects of public administration, such as the need for training in information technology is also evident. However the on-going political and constitutional instability in such societies makes the establishment of stable training programmes much more difficult.

New Public Management

The last two decades have witnessed a paradigm shift in the approach to public administration both as a field of study and an area of practice. Moreover the latter has been influenced by much of what has been published in the former. Academic students of Public Administration have historically interpreted what has been taking place in practice and developed critiques of the theories and concepts that have informed that practice. For example, Weberian theories of bureaucracy and organisation - for so long the lynch pin of thinking about, and the practice of modern management and administration - became the object of academic criticism in the 1970s which, in turn led to a reappraisal (i) of the values which underlie public service and (ii) of the role of government in modern society (see Scott and Thynne, 1994).

In recent years this dynamic relationship between theory and practice has led to a 're-focusing of the discipline' (Supra, vol. Ch. 1). Linked to widespread reform agendas which have grown out of what are often presented as new ideologies regarding the role of the state, and new strategies to fulfil that role, public administration has lurched towards a managerialist approach. This, in itself, has led to a vigorous academic debate between those who would at one extreme adopt a vigorously instrumental approach focused on the values of economy, effectiveness, efficiency and value for money, and those who argue for retention of the traditional orientation to public Administration education and training with its links to the academic discipline of political science and/or law.

This is not the place to enter into that debate but it is clear from some of the contributions in these two volumes that it is influencing many education and training programmes across the globe. It is equally evident however that it is not a debate that has penetrated the training institutions of some countries. It is hardly surprising that there has not been a universally uniform response to the managerialist debate. Its significance in any particularly society will depend on the configuration of local factors influencing the culture, the technological environment and the perceived need for change.

Our Canadian colleagues titled their contribution to this work 'plus ça change, plus c'est la même chose'- which may accurately depict the situation in relation to their particular debate about management and managerialism. However the more significant fact is that the academic and professional fraternity are holding the debate at all. Responses to current developments by those responsible for education and training programmes cannot be instant or all embracing. The adaptation of programmes must, by their nature, be incremental and piecemeal rather than radical and comprehensive. There is much evidence in these two volumes that our colleagues in universities and training institutes are engaged in the contemporary debates about public administration in their respective countries, that training programmes usually reflect the significant issues within the administration; that a healthy dynamic debate about the content of programmes, their mode of delivery and their immediate and overall objectives, is sustained in the majority of countries.

The picture that seems to be emerging is one in which those responsible for contemporary Public Administration education and training programmes are addressing the perennial dichotomy of keeping faith with the traditional norms, values and customs of their particular public services whilst at the same time responding to the pressures, demands and developments of the modern world. This conflict takes place whilst traditional norms and values may themselves be subject to significant swings in political favour, be it in South Africa or the Ukraine.

The result is that many training and education programmes vacillate between what have recently been described as a 'traditional paradigm' and a 'current paradigm', based respectively on a conservative elitist model and a modern collegial model of public administration (Zivanic, 1990). Each paradigm/model sees the role of the public administrator differently, requiring different skills, attitudes and values. Each is based on a different concept of how public administration should operate, what the dominant organisational culture should be, and how administrators should relate to the public and each other.

References

Hopper, M. (1990), 'Rattling SABRE - New Ways to Compete in Information', *Harvard Business Review*, May/June.

Ivanicevich, J.M. and Glueck, W.G. (1989), *Foundation of Personnel: Human Resources Management*, Irwin, Homewood, Illinois.

Lynn, N.B. and Wildawsky, A (eds), (1990) *Public Administration; the State of the Discipline*, Chatham House, New Jersey.

MacFarlane, W.F. (1984), 'Information Technology changes the way you compete', *Harvard Business Review*, May/June,14.

Milkovich, G.T. and Bondreau, G.T. and J.W. (1988), *Foundation of Personnel, Human Resource Management: a Diagnostic Approach*, Irwin, Homewood, Illinois.

Rouban, L. (1988), *The French Civil Service*, La Documentation Francaise, I I AP, Paris.

Scott, I and Thynne, I, (1994) Public Sector Reform: Critical Issues and Perspectives, *Asian Journal of Public Administration*, Hong Kong.

Silcock, R., in M.R.Davies et al (eds) (1998), *New State, New Millennium, New Public Management: Coping with the Problems of Transition: The Case of Slovenia*, University of Ljubljana U.N. (1996) *Handbook of Training in the Public Service*, UN publication, No. 66.

Ziller J. (1993), *Administration Comparées*, Montchrestien, Paris.

Zuvanic, L. (1990), 'Competencies Required for the Process of Change in Government: The Argentine Case' , paper delivered to IASIA, Paris.